Leading Economic Controversies

Leading Economic Controversies

EDWIN MANSFIELD
University of Pennsylvania

W. W. Norton & Company
NEW YORK   LONDON

ALL RIGHTS RESERVED
PRINTED IN THE UNITED STATES OF AMERICA

This book is composed in ITC Baskerville
Composition by Com Com
Manufacturing by Haddon Crafstmen

ISBN 0-393-97225-9 (pbk.)
W. W. Norton & Company, Inc.,
500 Fifth Avenue, New York, N.Y. 10110
http://www.wwnorton.com
W. W. Norton & Company Ltd.,
10 Coptic Street, London WC1A 1PU

3 4 5 6 7 8 9 0

To Beth and Ken

Contents

PART FOUR: **COMPETITION AND ANTITRUST POLICY**

PART FIVE: **THE ENVIRONMENT**

PART SIX: **FARM POLICY**

PART SEVEN: **GDP AND ECONOMIC GROWTH**

PART EIGHT: **FISCAL POLICY**

PART NINE: **TAXATION AND PERSONAL INVESTING**

PART TEN: **MONETARY POLICY**

PART ELEVEN: **INTERNATIONAL TRADE POLICY**

Preface

Economics is an exciting subject—or it can be if it is taught properly. Obviously, one of the most important purposes of an elementary economics course is to get students interested in the subject, and this can best be done by showing them how the principles of economics can enable them to understand better the major economic issues of today. That in brief is the purpose of the Fourth Edition of this book, which focuses on eleven central policy areas: (1) Social Security (2) education, (3) the distribution of income, (4) competition and antitrust policy, (5) the environment, (6) farm policy, (7) GDP and economic growth, (8) fiscal policy, (9) taxation and personal investing, (10) monetary policy, and (11) international trade policy. One-third of the articles included are new to this edition.

These policy areas play a major role in practically any elementary economics course. To arouse students' interest in each of these areas, this book presents contrasting (or in some cases, complementary) views by leading policymakers (like Alan Greenspan, and John Kasich), prominent scholars (like Robert Barro, Alan Blinder, Barry Bosworth, Robert Eisner, Robert Hall and Alvin Rabushka, Paul Krugman, Burton Malkiel, Charles Schultze, and James Tobin), and major business executives (like Robert Lutz), as well as government advisory groups like the President's Council of Economic Advisers. Each of the articles is at a level that is appropriate for the typical undergraduate. The articles, many of which are based on speeches, tend to be lighter in tone—and hence more palatable to students—than many other discussions of these issues. Also, it is worth noting that these articles tend to be very up-to-date.

In each of the eleven parts of this book, after the articles presenting different views of a particular issue, there are questions for analysis. These questions, which can form the basis for classroom discussion or homework exercises, are meant to provide an overview of the articles and to encourage the student to relate key points in the articles to the principles of economics.

This book was originally conceived as a supplement to *Economics U$A*, Fifth Edition, but many instructors have used it to supplement other elementary economics textbooks; and some have used it alone.

E.M.

October 1997

Leading Economic Controversies

PART ONE

SOCIAL SECURITY AND THE CONSUMER PRICE INDEX

Social Security payments are of great consequence to the aged and others in the United States. Thus it is not surprising that many citizens are worried about the government projections indicating that changes will have to be made in the Social Security system to maintain its solvency. The first article in this section, by President Clinton's Council of Economic Advisers, outlines the potential problems. The second article, by Barry Bosworth of the Brookings Institution discusses the findings of a panel of economists that the Consumer Price Index overstates inflation by about 1.1 percentage points annually. If this is true, Social Security payments could be lowered, thus making it less likely that major changes in the Social Security system would be required. However, Bosworth emphasizes that Congress should not "cede its responsibility to make critical public policy decisions to a group of putative experts."

Problems Ahead
for Social Security*

Janet Yellen,
Chair, Council of
Economic Advisers

PRESIDENT CLINTON'S COUNCIL
OF ECONOMIC ADVISERS

Without changing current law in any way, Social Security can pay full benefits well into the next century. Thereafter, without any changes in the structure of the program, funding will be sufficient to cover about 70 percent of benefits even 75 years from now. Nevertheless, the program faces a funding gap over the 75-year projection period and permanent imbalance after 75 years. The challenge is to restore balance to the program, raise national saving, and allow Social Security to continue to fulfill its many missions.

For almost 60 years, Social Security has provided elderly Americans with a basic level of retirement security. Currently, about 90 percent of "aged units"—married couples one of whom is aged 65 or older, and nonmarried persons aged 65 and over—get Social Security benefits. These benefits are the only form of retirement pension for about half of these households. Social Security is particularly important for the low-income elderly. For example, more than three-quarters of the money income (which includes earnings from work and interest, as well as retirement benefits) of households in the bottom two income quintiles comes from Social Security benefits. The comparable shares are about a quarter for the highest income quintile and about half for the second-highest.

*This is an excerpt from the *Economic Report of the President* (Washington, D.C.: Government Printing Office, 1997).

Social Security benefits keep some 15 million people above the poverty line and millions more from near poverty. As recently as 1959, when these data began to be collected, the poverty rate among the elderly was more than twice that for the rest of the adult population. Since then this rate has trended lower and is now slightly below that for other adults. Social Security has been a key factor behind this drop. Moreover, although the benefit schedule is progressive and some benefits are subject to partial taxation, Social Security benefits are not subject to an explicit means test. The lack of means testing allows many people to add other resources to their Social Security benefits and achieve a level of income not too far below that when they were working.

Social Security also provides protection against loss of family income due to disability or death. Roughly 5 million disabled adults and 3 million children receive monthly benefits; about half the children receiving benefits have lost one or both parents. In short, Social Security is an extremely valuable program that has raised the living standards of millions of Americans and markedly increased their sense of economic security by providing fully indexed annuities in the event of retirement, disability, or death of a breadwinner.

THE SIZE OF THE PROBLEM

In their annual report, the Trustees of the Social Security system publish projections of the system's revenues and outlays for the next 75 years. Three sets of projections are made, corresponding to three sets of assumptions about future levels of system costs. The intermediate cost projections in the 1996 report show that, from now through 2011, the Social Security system will bring in more money than it pays out. That is, payroll tax receipts plus receipts from income taxation of Social Security benefits will exceed outlays.

By that time the baby-boomers will have begun to retire, and growth in the labor force will slow, reflecting the decline in the fertility rate that occurred after 1960. The resulting increase in the ratio of retirees to workers will cause the outlays of the system to rise above taxes. In the relatively short period from 2012 through 2018, the annual interest income on assets in the Social Security trust funds will, together with tax receipts, produce enough revenues to cover benefit payments. After that, if no action is taken, total income will fall short of benefit payments, but the shortfall can be covered by drawing down trust fund assets until the funds are exhausted in 2029. Of course, the exhaustion of the trust funds does not mean the end of Social Security benefits. Even if no changes are made on the tax or the benefit side of the equation, payroll and benefit taxation at current rates will provide enough money to cover 75 percent of promised benefits in 2040 and nearly 70 percent in 2070.

The Politics of Immaculate Conception*

BARRY BOSWORTH

L ast December the Advisory Commission to Study the Consumer Price Index issued a report arguing that the CPI has been overstating inflation for the past few decades—by 1.1 percent in recent years. The commission recommended that the overstatement be corrected forthwith.

Years of neglect and underfunding have seriously eroded the quality of the U.S. statistical system, and the commission's attention to the adequacy of the CPI as a measure of inflation is welcome. But the accuracy of national statistics was not the only issue Congress had in mind when it appointed the commission. Adjusting the CPI in accord with the commission's recommendation would have major effects on taxes, federal benefits, and the goal of future budget balance.

The commission's conclusion that the CPI overstates inflation was not surprising. It is consistent with earlier research on the price indexes, and few analysts would disagree. But there is less empirical basis for the commission's estimate of the magnitude of the bias. While the estimate is consistent with a number of recent survey articles, it is important to understand that all the reports are extrapolating from a common small set of empirical studies, none of which was intended to provide an unbiased as-

*This article appeared in the *Brookings Review* in Spring 1997. Barry Bosworth is a senior fellow at the Brookings Institution.

sessment. The empirical studies, most arising from research conducted at the Bureau of Labor Statistics, focused on specific problems with the CPI—and, naturally, on those areas of the CPI where the effect would be largest. At this time, we do not know the extent to which the results of studies of those narrow areas can be generalized to other parts of the index.

The issue of bias in the CPI involves both technical aspects of constructing an index and measures of quality change. The technical issues are straightforward, and the commission estimates their impact on the rate of change in the CPI at 0.5 percent per year. The commission has highlighted some basic problems and provided specific suggestions that would help resolve them. Congress should provide the funding to update the index, and the BLS should move in the direction proposed by the commission. The result would be a better index.

The problems with the commission's recommendations arise in connection with the issue of quality change, the remaining 0.6 percentage point of overstatement. In the first place, the commission's report fails to reflect fully the extent to which the current CPI already adjusts for quality change. Of course the quality of some goods and services has improved. But that is not the point. The real question is whether the quality improvements have been more than are embodied in the current procedures. For, though few people outside the BLS seem to know it, the index already reflects a large amount of quality gain. In 1995 the total price increase in a subsample of the CPI, covering about 70 percent of the total, amounted to 4.7 percent. But the BLS determined that 2.6 percentage points, or slightly over half the increase, represented improvements in quality. That is, quality improvements offset about half of the gross price increase, yielding an estimated 2.2 percent inflation rate.

The CPI commission is arguing that the quality adjustment should have been 0.6 percentage points larger, 3.2 percent rather than 2.6 percent. They could be correct, but on the basis of existing evidence, we don't know that. I don't see how anyone can be that precise. Indeed, one disappointing feature of the commission's report is that it offers no new procedures to improve the estimate of quality change; it simply asserts that it is larger than estimated by the BLS.

Much of the dispute arises out of different views of how producers go about introducing price and quality changes. If most quality changes are small and incremental in nature, current BLS techniques may overlook them and end up misstating the price change. But if price and quality changes are tied closely together in the introduction of new models, the BLS methodology may overestimate quality improvements and understate inflation, a possibility ignored by the commission. In most cases, major changes in a product's characteristics will result in its being dropped from

CHART 1 Low-income Population by Age, Actual and Simulated, 1995

Percentage below current poverty income level

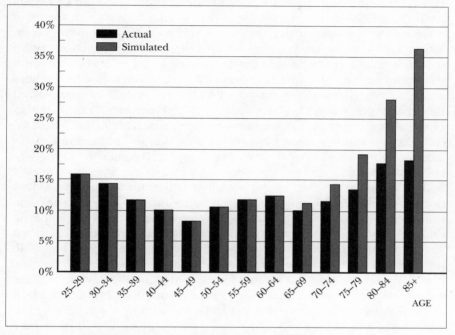

Source: Calculated from March 1996 CPS using poverty level as measure of low income.

the index, implicitly attributing most of any price change to quality. Thus, price increases that are imbedded in new models are ignored and assumed equal to those of other products in that month. On average, a product's characteristics will undergo major change every two years.

In addition, the commission argues that the CPI should be an index of the cost of living and not just the average cost of a fixed market basket of goods and services. That seems right in concept. A cost of living index would reflect the fact that consumers can avoid some price increases by switching to substitute products. But pushing that idea to the extreme can open a can of worms that exceeds the capacity of the current methodology. Where do we draw the line between economic and noneconomic aspects of the cost of living, and are they separable? How should we value the time required to shop for the lowest price and increases in the range of consumer choices?

Congress is drawn to the issue not out of a fascination with the arcane issues of index number construction, but because the CPI is used to adjust large elements of the federal budget—Social Security benefits and income tax brackets—for annual increases in the cost of living. A revised CPI offers an "immaculate conception" version of deficit reduction in which spending is cut without Congress taking the blame. While the first-year savings from a lower CPI would be small, they build up over time. A 1.1 percentage point reduction in the annual increment to the CPI would save $150 billion in the tenth year, or about 1 percent of the GDP. It is becoming evident, however, that procedural changes by the BLS will generate only a fraction of the commission's suggested overestimate of 1.1 percent. Thus, it is suggested that a group of "experts" who are knowledgeable of the actual increase in the nation's average cost of living could provide Congress with a more accurate measure, again providing Congress with some cover for benefit reductions.

Were it not for the politics of immaculate conception, I don't think that Congress would be considering this particular form of benefit reduction. Consider, for example, its impact on the nation's oldest citizens. The typical retiree can expect to receive Social Security benefits for about 20 years. The importance of these benefits rises with age: private pensions have no inflation adjustment and retirees tend to use up their own assets. The proposed adjustment to the CPI would have no effect on the benefit of a new retiree, but benefits in each succeeding year would rise by a smaller percentage. After 10 years, benefits would be reduced by about 12 percent; after 20 years, by 25 percent. Currently, the average income of those over age 80 is only two-thirds that of people aged 65–69, and the poverty rate rises from 10 percent for families with a head aged 65–69 to 18 percent for those over age 80. The recommendation of the commission would exacerbate that trend. If the recommendation had been in effect for the past two decades, the proportion of those aged 65–69 with income below the current poverty standard would rise only marginally to 11 percent, but for those over age 80 it would soar above 30 percent.

Congress will have to scale back Social Security benefits in future years, but it should consider carefully the implications of how it makes the cuts. It makes far more sense to concentrate the cuts at the beginning of the retirement period when individuals can mitigate their effect by postponing retirement or working part-time, not when retirees are in their 80s and have no employment options. Nor should Congress cede its responsibility to make critical public policy decisions to a group of putative experts. Unless they are expert shoppers, it is not at all clear what they are supposed to know about annual changes in the cost of living that cannot be incorporated in the procedures of the BLS.

QUESTIONS FOR ANALYSIS

1. Have Social Security benefits played a role in lowering the poverty rate among the elderly?

2. Is there likely to be an increase in the ratio of retirees to workers? What effect is this likely to have?

3. What was the conclusion of the Advisory Commission to Study the Consumer Price Index?

4. Does Barry Bosworth agree with the Advisory Commission to Study the Consumer Price Index that, because of changes in the quality of goods, the Consumer Price Index overstates the inflation rate by about 0.6 percentage points per year?

5. According to Bosworth, the recommendations of the commission would increase the percentage of people over 80 with incomes below the poverty line. Why?

6. Bosworth argues that Congress should not cede its responsibility to make critical public policy decisions to "experts." Do you agree? Why or why not?

PART TWO

EDUCATION

There is general agreement among economists and others that education is of great importance to the U.S. economy. In the first article, the Council of Economic Advisers emphasizes that, "rather than continue to debate how much of a difference [additional resources devoted to education] have made in the past, we should be asking how programs and incentives could be structured today to ensure even greater benefits from resources invested now and in the future." In the next article, Charles Schultze, senior fellow at the Brookings Institution, concludes that: "The evidence is overwhelming that the quality of American elementary and secondary education leaves much to be desired and that the level of American productivity and living standards has been and will continue to be lowered by that deterioration in quality."

The Payoff to Public Investment in Education*

Alicia H. Munnell, member, Council of Economic Advisers

PRESIDENT CLINTON'S COUNCIL OF ECONOMIC ADVISERS

S ince the publication of *Equality of Educational Opportunity* (commonly known as the Coleman Report) in 1966, researchers have struggled with the question of whether increased expenditure on schools improves student performance. The debate is often quite contentious because of the large differences in expenditure per pupil between rich and poor school districts. For example, during the 1992–93 school year, New Jersey spent more than $9,400 per pupil in public elementary and secondary schools, while Alabama and Mississippi spent less than $3,900. Regional differences in the cost of living can explain only a small part of such variation. Furthermore, given the importance of local financing of public education, expenditure per pupil can differ by a factor of two or three even between districts in the same State.

Typically, analysts compare average test scores in high-spending and low-spending districts to learn about the effect of additional resources on scores. Not surprisingly, the high-spending districts have higher average scores. However, since high-spending districts also tend to have higher average family income and parental education, the differences in student performance may be caused not by differences in the level of spending but

*This is an excerpt from the *Economic Report of the President* (Washington, D.C.: Government Printing Office, 1996).

13

by differences in family resources. When analysts compare test scores in high- and low-spending districts with similar family incomes and parental education, the results are often considered provocative: districts that spend more are often found *not* to have higher test scores.

However, additional resources could have other beneficial impacts. The standardized tests used in much of the research may not reliably measure the kinds of improvements that parents or policymakers would expect schools to produce with additional resources. The benefits of new courses in American history, geometry, or calculus or improved learning opportunities for the disabled—valuable as they may be—would not be captured by such measures.

Consistent with this hypothesis, studies of the long-term impacts of school expenditure on earnings and educational attainment—in contrast to those that focus on test scores—yield more optimistic evidence that public investment in elementary and secondary schooling does generate benefits later in students' lives. For instance, better paid and better educated teachers and smaller classroom size have been associated with greater educational attainment and higher payoffs to education later in life, even if they have not had large effects on the particular test scores used. One recent study concluded that the payoff was not only positive but financially lucrative: a 10 percent increase in expenditures from kindergarten through 12th grade would produce additional lifetime earnings valued at 1.2 times the additional cost (in present value terms). Admittedly, studies of this kind remain few, and some authors have reported less positive results, but some evidence suggests that past increases in spending on education did bear fruit, even if the results did not register on the particular tests used.

But the debate over such findings often misses a more relevant question: rather than continue to debate how much of a difference additional resources have made in the past, we should be asking how programs and incentives could be structured today to ensure even greater benefits from resources invested now and in the future. It is difficult to believe that a knowledgeable school principal could not find a way to use additional resources to improve student learning, as long as the incentives in the environment rewarded such gains. The task of policymakers should be to create an environment in which incentives dictate that resources be invested profitably.

On this question, Federal, State, and local governments are already a step ahead of the academic debate. Many of the educational reforms being pursued today seek to produce more decentralization and greater accountability, both of which are designed to create an environment in which resources are used more efficiently. The charter school movement is a good example. Minnesota was the first State to pass a law allowing for charter schools in 1991. Since then 19 other States have enacted laws permitting the development of charter schools. A charter school is usually the brain-child of a committed group of teachers or set of parents who want the flex-ibility to try a different approach. Typically, they apply to the local school board or the State department of education for a charter allowing them to open a new school with public funding. Since charter schools are public schools, they do not charge tuition. Such charters typically waive many of the regulatory requirements imposed on other public schools for 3 to 5 years, at which time they are subject to review.

Charter schools enhance accountability in two ways. First, charter con-tracts often specify benchmarks for performance, such as scores on specific state assessments. In exchange for the freedom to innovate, charter school organizers are expected to produce results. Some contracts are more spe-cific in spelling out such performance expectations than others. As states develop better assessment tools under the Goals 2000: Educate America Act, these performance expectations can be more explicitly stated. Second, the presence of charter schools is intended to encourage innovation by nearby public and private schools, through the demonstration of successful educational strategies and through the threat of lost enrollment.

The Department of Education has helped to nurture the charter school movement by providing seed money for the establishment of charter schools. In the 1995 fiscal year, the Federal Government provided nearly $6 million in grants to help cover startup costs for charter schools. The Ad-ministration hopes to increase this commitment significantly over the next few years.

But the establishment of charter schools represents only one way in which States and local school districts are seeking to provide better incen-tives for schools and teachers. School report cards, performance bonuses for schools, magnet schools, and other forms of public school choice are also being tested.

Publicly funded vouchers for use at private schools are another, more radical approach. But vouchers have several problems. Their advocates fail to recognize the many ways in which education for children differs from conventional goods. The primary risk of vouchers is that they may produce a dramatic increase in social stratification. The cost in terms of the result-ing damage to social mobility and social cohesion could exceed any benefit in terms of better school performance. Because they are public schools de-pendent upon public support, charter schools can be more carefully planned to serve all children's interests by locating them in urban areas, by insisting on open admissions policies, by holding them directly account-able for results, and—when oversubscribed—by requiring them to estab-lish lotteries for admission. Charter schools provide a framework for an improved educational system, with parents and teachers working together to develop new and creative solutions to the challenges they face, and demanding accountability of all participants in the educational process.

Some approaches to accountability are better suited to some environments than others. For instance, school report cards are better indicators of school performance when mobility between schools is low and when one can control for differences in student characteristics. Charter schools and magnet schools provide better incentives when the quality of local transportation is good and parents are engaged and well informed. Still another approach, which several European countries employ, raises the stakes for students, through more widespread use of achievement tests as a criterion for high school graduation and college admission, or even by employers in their hiring decisions (Box 1). Given the diversity of circumstances around the country, it is appropriate that each State and school district pursue its own strategy for encouraging more decentralization and accountability.

BOX 1   **RAISING THE STAKES FOR STUDENTS**

Despite recent gains, American youth continue to perform poorly in science and mathematics relative to their counterparts in many other industrialized countries. American students also seem to spend less time on their studies than students in other countries. The Organization for Economic Cooperation and Development has suggested that one of the causes of the poorer U.S. performance is the lack of connection between high school achievement and employment or schooling opportunities.

Unless they are planning to attend a selective college, high school students in America often have little incentive to do well academically. Surveys suggest that employers have difficulty collecting and interpreting transcripts from many different schools. And except for the most competitive colleges, a student's performance in high school has little impact on his or her chances of admission to college. The skills developed in school may well matter later in students' careers, but many students may fail to see a connection between performance in school and immediate prospects for a job or college admission.

In contrast, many European countries require students graduating from high school to take tests in various subject areas. Universities use these scores in making admission decisions, as do employers in their hiring decisions. Some precedent for such high-stakes testing exists in the United States—the Regents Examination in New York is an example. By raising the stakes for high school performance—or, possibly more important, making the actual consequences more visible—these tests may induce students to work harder.

An achievement test may also strengthen the incentives of students and teachers to work together. Absent an external standard, schools judge individual students relative to their classmates. But the relative scale gives students an incentive to discourage their peers from "wrecking the curve." In contrast, an external standard unites teachers, students, and their classmates in a common objective: to perform well.

Education: A Memo to the President*

CHARLES SCHULTZE

Those who have studied the sources of economic growth agree that increases in the educational qualifications of the American labor force have contributed greatly to the growth in its productivity. The importance of education to productivity growth can also be observed in other countries—the education of a country's work force is an important determinant of its output and income per worker.

THE EDUCATION AND SKILLS OF THE LABOR FORCE

Growth studies rely on the central assumption that economic payoff to education—the higher productivity associated with additional years of education—can be measured by examining the differences in earnings among people with different amounts of education. In the late 1970s, for example, average incomes of full-time (male) workers varied according to years of school completed, as shown in Table 1. The number of years of school completed by American workers has been growing steadily since the country was founded. That growth has continued throughout the postwar period. Using data like that shown in Table 1, Edward Denison

*Charles Schultze is a senior fellow at the Brookings Institution. This article comes from his *Memos to the President* (Washington, D.C.: Brookings, 1992).

TABLE 1 Income Disparity by Years of Schooling

EDUCATION	RATIO
High school dropout	0.84
High school graduate	1.00
1–4 years of college	1.48
5 or more years of college	1.68

found that between 1929 and 1982 the increase in schooling accounted for some 0.4 percent a year of the 1.6 percent annual growth rate in productivity.[1] Moreover, that 0.4 percent a year contribution of education was roughly the same in all the major subperiods, including the years after 1973. The recent productivity slowdown cannot be attributed to a trailing off in the growth of years of schooling among American workers. Other researchers, using more detailed data and some refinements of technique, basically confirm these findings.

The traditional growth studies have relied on data about the quantity of education, as measured by years of school completed. But what about quality? It is widely believed that in recent years the quality of American education has deteriorated. Scores on the Scholastic Aptitude Test (SAT) started a long period of decline after the mid-1960s. Students born in 1945 and tested in 1963 achieved an average score (math plus verbal) of 980. Seventeen years later, in 1980, the cohort of students born in 1962 and tested in 1980 averaged a score of only 890, a 10 percent decline. Could that not be at least one cause of the productivity slowdown?

Most of those who have carefully investigated the question concluded that the decline in educational test scores was unlikely to have been significantly responsible for the slowdown in productivity growth *to date*. It has been estimated that about half of the decline in the SAT scores (and all of the decline before 1973) occurred because an increasing proportion of the high school population was taking them; the tests were reaching further and further down into the ability pool, and quite naturally the average declined. More important, the decline in test scores that began in the late 1960s affected only new entrants to the labor force, and those entrants weren't a large enough proportion of the whole labor force to have been associated with the decline in productivity growth that began occurring in the late 1960s and became worse in the 1970s. Finally, the slowdown in pro-

[1] Edward F. Denison, *Trends in American Economic Growth, 1929–82* (Brookings, 1985), p. 114.

ductivity growth was a worldwide phenomenon and occurred in countries whose educational performance is constantly being held up as examples of success.

Recently, a careful study by John Bishop of Cornell University has suggested that the drop in SAT scores may adversely affect productivity in the future.[2] In the first place, the evidence strongly suggests that prior to the late 1960s the general intellectual achievement of American students, as measured by various tests, had been rising steadily at least since the turn of the century. The evidence also shows that improved intellectual achievement is associated with higher wages and higher productivity. Thus some fraction of the growth in American productivity before 1970 depended on a continuing rise in the quality of education and the intellectual level of the American work force (aside from the improvement simply because of increased years of schooling). To the extent that average test scores measure intellectual achievement—and to a significant extent they do—simply maintaining the earlier (pre-1970s) growth rate of productivity would have required continued improvement in test scores. The decline in scores that occurred after the late 1960s was thus more serious than appears at first glance.

In the decade of the 1970s the downturn in test scores of new entrants to the labor force did not play a large role in the reduction of productivity growth, simply because—as noted above—those young workers formed such a small segment of the overall work force. But, as Bishop warns, the fraction of workers whose test scores fall below the earlier trend is steadily growing as more and more of the work force consists of cohorts of workers who graduated from school after the late 1960s. Even if the recent recovery in test scores continues and represents a real improvement in intellectual achievement, scores will remain for a very long time below the point they would have been had the trends of the 1950s and 1960s been sustained. Thus Bishop calculates that even on the optimistic assumption of continued recovery, the average quality and productivity of the work force in 1990 was 3.6 percent below where earlier trends would have put it, and by the year 2000 the quality shortfall will be 5.5 percent. That's a huge amount. It means a loss of about $250 billion in GNP below its earlier growth path. Although these estimates probably exaggerate the effect of the fall in test scores—it may be unreasonable to have expected the 1950s and 1960s improvements to continue forever—the evidence is strong enough to establish the distinct likelihood that test scores do measure intellectual achievement, even if imperfectly; that improved intellectual achievement

[2]John Bishop, "Is the Test Score Decline Responsible for the Productivity Growth Decline?" *American Economic Review*, vol. 79 (March 1989), pp. 178–97.

of the labor force is associated with productivity growth; and that the post-1960s decline in test scores will be increasingly damping the growth of American productivity, even if some recovery in scores takes place.

BUSINESS PRACTICES AND THE QUALITY OF ELEMENTARY AND SECONDARY EDUCATION

Not only has the apparent intellectual achievement of American high school students declined, but a volume of evidence has accumulated indicating that American elementary and secondary students are not nearly as well prepared as their counterparts in other advanced countries. The American educational system has some advantages over those of many other countries, especially in encouraging independent thinking and innovation. But in imparting knowledge and skills, especially in math and science, American education prepared students far less well than the school systems of many other countries. On standardized tests, American students score much lower than do students of similar age in foreign countries, and the discrepancy seems to grow as the students advance through the elementary and secondary school system. As the most egregious example, the test scores of American students at the end of high school were four grade equivalents behind those of Japanese students with the same number of years in school. But American students at the high school and elementary levels also score poorly compared with students in virtually all other advanced countries. In almost none of the comparisons can the poor U.S. results be explained by the phenomenon that a larger fraction of U.S. students finish high school than is the case in other countries. In a recent report, the National Science Foundation summed up the evidence this way: "Thus, U.S. 10-year-old students in science ranked in the middle of the countries, lost ground by age 14, and scored at or near the bottom by the 12th grade."[3]

There is some reason to believe that those American students who attend college—at least the better four-year colleges—begin to catch up to their foreign counterparts. Certainly competition is intense among foreign students to attend the top American institutions of higher learning. But approximately half of the young people graduating from high school do not go to college; the other half enter the labor force directly from high school.

Over the years, scores of studies have documented the relationship between what a worker scores on tests measuring competence and subsequent productivity in the workplace. Research conducted for the armed

[3]National Science Board, *Science and Engineering Indicators—1989* (Washington: Government Printing Office, 1989), p. 28.

forces amply demonstrates the same point. There is clearly a cost to the nation, in forgone productivity and income, that can be associated with the low intellectual achievement of the average American worker who has recently entered the work force after high school.

The same John Bishop cited above has identified at least one potentially removable cause for the poor performance record of American high school students.[4] He assembled a large body of evidence that shows that despite the positive relationship between the productivity of young workers (who have not attended college) and prior educational achievement, there is little connection between the earnings of young male workers during the first five to ten years of work and their educational achievement, and only small gains for young women. For those students not going on to college, there are thus few economic incentives to do well in high school and to score well on performance tests. And, on average, American high school students, not surprisingly, spend a much smaller share of their time in school and are commonly believed to do less homework than their foreign counterparts.

James Rosenbaum of Northwestern University points out that college-bound students have substantial incentives to perform well in high school, and their teachers and administrators have incentives to promote that objective.[5] These incentives are effectively enforced by the colleges who penalize poor work and reward good performance. But for students not aspiring to college, the performance incentives are lacking for student and teacher, because future job and income prospects are not related to school performance. As Rosenbaum notes, a tacit conspiracy exists among students and teachers—if you don't hassle me, I won't hassle you.

Why do employers ignore the positive relationship between prior student achievement and high productivity? Why don't the better students get the better jobs and earn the higher wages? The answers are not entirely clear, but Bishop suggests some probable ones. Although tests are available for measuring performance, though imperfectly, in basic language, math, and other skills, concern over potential racial bias led the Equal Employment Opportunity Commission to issue guidelines in 1971 that led to a sharp decline in the tests' subsequent use by employers. Moreover, unlike the high schools in many other countries, most U.S. high schools do not provide transcripts and teachers' referrals to potential employers. And fi-

[4]John Bishop, "Incentives for Learning: Why American High School Students Compare So Poorly to Their Counterparts Overseas," in Commission on Workforce Quality and Labor Market Efficiency, *Investing in People: A Strategy to Address America's Workforce Crisis*, Background Papers, vol. 1 (Department of Labor, 1989).

[5]James E. Rosenbaum, "What If Good Jobs Depended on Good Grades?" *American Educator*, vol. 13 (Winter 1989), pp. 10–15, 40–42.

nally, as Harvard's Richard Murnane suggests, many of the widely used tests do not measure problem solving ability at all well, and problem solving ability is the most important skill in the workplace.[6] Since there is a tendency to teach to tests, students are not well prepared or tested for precisely those traits that will be most useful to them in the workplace.

THE ECONOMIC CONSEQUENCES OF THE EDUCATIONAL SHORTFALL

A sharp increase in the inequality of income has accompanied the slow growth of the American economy since the early 1970s. As we have already seen, after 1973 average family income grew very slowly. Furthermore, the income of the bottom 40 percent of families fell, while income for the top 20 percent, and even more striking, for the top 5 percent, grew handsomely. Perhaps the most important aspect of that rising income inequality is the widening gap between the wages of the college educated and the wages of workers, especially young ones, with a high school or less than high school education. Thus, a recent study by Frank Levy found that in 1986 the average annual earnings of a male, aged twenty-five to thirty-four, with four years of high school were 16 percent lower than they were in 1973 (after adjustment for inflation), while the earnings of the average college graduate were approximately unchanged.[7] Even more dramatically, another study that examined changes in wages for high- and low-paid employees found that by 1990 the wages of the bottom 20 percent of American workers (the lowest paid and presumably the least educated and the least skilled) had fallen some 25 to 30 percent below the point they had been in 1973.[8] Harvard's Richard Freeman and some of his colleagues have estimated that only a modest fraction (20 to 30 percent) of the fall in the relative wages of the less educated took place because of loss of high-paying semiskilled jobs in manufacturing industries such as steel and autos.[9] Rather, it principally reflected an across-the-board decline in wages of the less educated and less skilled in all industries. Moreover, the lower earnings did not reflect a shift in job creation in American industry toward low-skill and away from high-skill jobs. If that had been true, there would have been

---

[6]Richard J. Murnane, "Education and the Productivity of the Work Force: Looking Ahead," in Robert E. Litan, Robert Z. Lawrence, and Charles L. Schultze, eds., *American Living Standards: Threats and Challenges* (Brookings, 1988), pp. 215–45.

[7]Frank Levy, "Incomes," in Lawrence and Schultze, *American Living Standards,* pp. 108–53.

[8]Chinhui Juhn, Kevin Murphy, and Robert Topel, "Why Has the Natural Rate of Unemployment Increased over Time?" *Brookings Papers on Economic Activity 2:* 1991, pp. 75–133.

[9]McKinley L. Blackburn, David E. Bloom, and Richard B. Freeman, "The Declining Economic Position of Less Skilled American Men," in Gary Burtless, ed., *A Future of Lousy Jobs? The Changing Structure of U.S. Wages* (Brookings, 1990), pp. 31–67.

a surplus of the college educated and a shortage of less well-educated workers, and the relative wages of the college educated population would have been bid down relative to the wages of the high school educated, rather than up as was the case. The problem, in short, is not a scarcity of skilled jobs but a shortage of skilled workers.

It may well be true that no absolute decline has occurred in the educational accomplishments and skills of those entering the labor force out of high school. But as technology advances, American industry and other business firms are increasing the technological sophistication and the skill requirements in the workplace. Unless the average level of skills and problem solving capabilities among the high-school educated work force continually improves, employers are increasingly forced to downgrade the skill content, the productivity, and the wages of many jobs at the lower end of the skill distribution.

The problem of educational quality is made more acute by the increasing globalization of modern production. As transportation costs have fallen around the world, and multinational firms have invested heavily in the rapidly developing countries of the Pacific rim and elsewhere, American workers compete far more often with a worldwide industrial labor force. The old sources of comparative advantage, abundant raw materials and cheap capital, have become much less important, while the human skills of management and workers in mastering high-quality, technologically advanced methods of production, transportation, distribution, and finance have become much more important. Markets for American goods and services produced by skilled, competent, and well-educated workers are expanding rapidly, and international trade is a force boosting the wages of such workers. But correspondingly, American workers with low skills and poor education are increasingly competing with the work force of lower-income but rapidly industrializing countries.

A country whose educational and training institutions continued to improve the skills of one-half of its new labor force entrants (college and post-college graduates) while holding constant the skills of the remainder would experience a growing maldistribution of income in the absence of any world trade. But that result will be even more striking as economic and technological developments internationalize world markets. This wave of developments will not recede. Improved education and skill training, not protection, is the answer.

POLICY RESPONSES

The evidence is overwhelming that the quality of American elementary and secondary education leaves much to be desired and that the level of American productivity and living standards has been and will continue to be lowered by that deterioration in quality. The discipline of economics does not offer specific proposals to deal with this problem. But it can provide a few tips. In particular, economics stresses the importance of incentives.

Incentives for Students

John Bishop, correctly I think, has put his finger on one serious problem and pointed in the general direction of what might be done to improve the situation. Employers should be able to reward previous achievement at the high school level by assigning jobs and wage levels on the basis of that performance as indicated by grades and achievement test results, in turn creating some incentives, which apparently do not now exist, for young people to do better in high school even when they are not going on to college. The federal government could sponsor the research and validation needed to improve existing tests, or design and validate new ones, that better measure future performance for white and minority youth. Emphasis should be on testing for problem solving skills. In a related vein, those states that do not have standardized statewide tests should adopt the requirement that all schools administer them. With the states, the federal government could help develop the institutional framework and the privacy protection that would make it feasible for employers, even small- and medium-sized ones, to request and receive in timely fashion high school grades and standardized test scores from high schools, for job applicants (with, of course, the consent of the applicant).

Incentives for Schools

Better incentives in the form of a future wage payoff from good performance should motivate students to put forth more effort. Schools and teachers also need better incentives. It is not the province of economics to design incentives for educational institutions. Nevertheless, the logic of economics would generally favor suggestions, which have been put forward recently, urging the decentralization of local systems, eliminating large slices of central educational bureaucracies, giving more power to principals and teachers in individual schools, and in particular providing parents with the right of choice among individual schools.[10] While the analogy with the marketplace is far from perfect and should not be pushed to the limit, economic history and analysis strongly confirm the benefits for consumers of having vigorous competition among the providers of consumer services

---

[10]See John E. Chubb and Terry M. Moe, *Politics, Markets, and America's Schools* (Brookings, 1990).

and can attest to the spur to performance imparted by the threat of loss of markets.

Finally, in considering these matters, one must bear in mind the simple arithmetic of schools and labor markets. Realistically, better incentives for students and schools and other improvements in educational quality would only begin to affect the performance of high school graduates some years down the pike. In turn, each year's cohort of new workers represents only about 2 to 3 percent of the total labor force. Thus, even educational improvements set in motion immediately would not reach half of the labor force until after the year 2020. And so we should consider means to upgrade the skills of today's adult workers. In the end, hard-headed analysis may indicate little promise for a large-scale effort to educate adult workers. But it would be a mistake to neglect this possibility in the absence of such a negative finding.

QUESTIONS FOR ANALYSIS

1. How much difference do additional resources have on test scores?

2. What are the advantages of charter schools?

3. Do you favor publicly funded vouchers for use at private schools? Why or why not?

4. If they are not planning to attend a selective college, do high school students have much incentive to do well academically?

5. Is there evidence that the quality of U.S. education has deteriorated in recent years?

6. Are U.S. elementary and secondary students as well prepared as their counterparts in other countries?

7. As technology advances, U.S. industry is increasing the technological sophistication and the skill requirements in the workplace. If the average level of skill among the high-school-educated workforce does not improve, what will happen to the wages of many jobs at the lower end of the skill distribution?

8. What role do incentives play? How can they be improved?

PART THREE

THE

DISTRIBUTION

OF INCOME

Two of the big concerns of the mid-1990s have been the relatively slow rate of growth of real income in the United States and the growing inequality of incomes, but there has been considerable debate about what these trends mean and don't mean. The first article, by President Clinton's Council of Economic Advisers, attributes the slow growth of real income to a slowdown in productivity growth and the increase in inequality to increasing returns to education and experience. The second article, by the Republican members of the Joint Economic Committee of Congress, attacks some of the statistical evidence used to support the proposition that income inequality has increased. The third article, by Robert Barro of Harvard University, discusses the effects of the 1993 increases in marginal tax rates on the rich.

Slowing Wage Growth and Widening Inequality*

Laura D'Andrea Tyson,
former Chair, Council of
Economic Advisers

PRESIDENT CLINTON'S COUNCIL OF ECONOMIC ADVISERS*

In the last two decades, family income growth has stagnated and incomes have become more unequally distributed. In fact, the real incomes of the bottom 60 percent of American families were lower in the early 1990s than for the analogous families at the end of the 1970s. Underlying the rising disparity in the fortunes of American families has been a rise in labor market inequality that has shifted wage and employment opportunities in favor of the more educated and the more experienced. Less educated workers suffered substantial losses in real earnings during the 1980s. Here we consider the dimensions, and some likely causes, of slow income growth and widening inequality.

SLOW INCOME GROWTH

Income trends have been discouraging for about two decades—the median family today has virtually the same real income as the median family 20

*This is an excerpt from the *Economic Report of the President* (Washington, DC: Government Printing Office, 1994).

CHART 1   Real Hourly Compensation and Wages

The growth of real compensation per hour and of real hourly wages has declined since 1973.

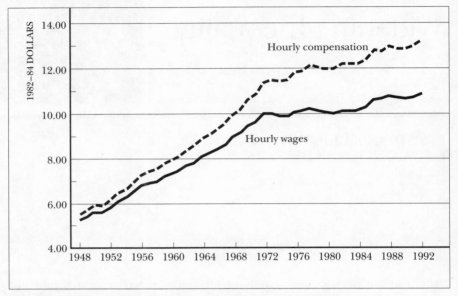

Note: Compensation and average hourly earnings deflated by CPI-U-X1.

Sources: Department of Commerce and Department of Labor.

years ago. This stagnation is a marked departure from the substantial income growth that occurred over previous generations.

From 1947 to 1973 the real income of the median American family increased by a robust 2.8 percent a year, more than doubling. In contrast, from 1973 to 1992 the income of the typical American family was essentially stagnant, rising by only 0.1 percent a year after adjusting for inflation. (The trend from 1979 to 1989—roughly equivalent years in the economic cycle—is similar.) At the pace of income growth from 1973 to 1992, it would take centuries for real median family income to double.

Although the labor force participation decisions of women and changes in the composition of families have affected family income, the major trends in family income are dominated by trends in real wages. Chart 1 shows the changes in wages and total hourly compensation, adjusted for inflation, since 1948. Both wages and compensation suffered abrupt slowdowns in growth rates around 1973.

BOX 1 **GROWING INEQUALITY OF EMPLOYMENT AND UNEMPLOYMENT**

The falling relative wages of those with less experience and schooling may explain, at least in part, some of the observed changes in employment-to-population ratios for certain demographic groups. The black and teenage populations tend to have less schooling than the average for all Americans. Consequently, the wages they command have fallen, making work less attractive. To the extent that the shift in demand away from less-educated workers is manifest in fewer available jobs instead of lower wages, these groups face higher unemployment rates as well.

GROWING INEQUALITY

Families have been affected unevenly by recent income trends. Real incomes at the top have increased smartly, real incomes at the middle have essentially stagnated, and real incomes at the bottom have fallen. Box 1 discusses the implications of these developments for employment and unemployment.

From 1973 to 1992, the average real income of the upper 20 percent of families rose 19 percent, or about 1 percent per year. This is well below the rate for the 1950s and 1960s, but far better than for the rest of the population. Between 1973 and 1992, the average income of the middle 20 percent of families rose a paltry 4 percent in real terms. Lower income families fared even worse. Among the bottom 20 percent of families, mean real income fell by 12 percent from 1973 to 1992. Chart 2 shows the growth of mean family incomes for different income groups over the periods before and after 1973. It makes clear just how abrupt the changes in the distribution of income growth have been. A trend toward greater equality in the 1960s and toward greater inequality in the 1970s and 1980s is apparent in both income and consumption measures of economic well-being. Rising inequality of family incomes during the 1980s is apparent in both pretax and posttax income measures.

EXPLAINING SLOW WAGE GROWTH

Stagnant wages and slow total compensation growth since the early 1970s largely reflect a substantial slowdown in productivity growth. [Productivity is defined as output per hour of labor.] From 1947 to 1973 productivity rose at a compound annual rate of 3.1 percent, and inflation-adjusted compensation per hour grew at a similar rate. From 1973 to 1979 the rate of productivity growth fell to an average of 0.8 percent a year, and compensation growth fell with it. Since 1979 the productivity growth rate has picked

CHART 2 Average Annual Growth of Mean Family Income by Income Quintile

Family incomes in all income groups grew more or less evenly, but slightly faster for lower income groups, before 1973.

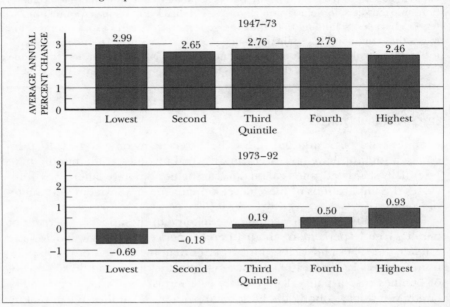

Source: Department of Commerce.

up only slightly, averaging 1.2 percent on an annual basis. [There is a] close relation between productivity and real compensation. Boxes 2 and 3 discuss some of the other effects of productivity growth.

The productivity slowdown has been intensely studied. Many partial explanations have been given, but no complete accounting has been made.

EXPLAINING THE GROWTH OF INEQUALITY

Several factors have contributed to widening inequality. One major factor is increasing returns to education and experience. The college–high school wage premium increased by over 100 percent for workers aged 25 to 34 between 1974 and 1992, while increasing 20 percent for all workers 18 years old and over. In addition, among workers without college degrees, the average wages of older workers increased relative to those of younger workers. Since the relative supply of educated workers has increased at the same time that wage disparities have grown, the demand for educated workers must have increased faster than their supply. Some have suggested

CHART 3 Productivity Growth and Price Reductions, 1950–90

Productivity growth in an industry leads to lower relative prices.

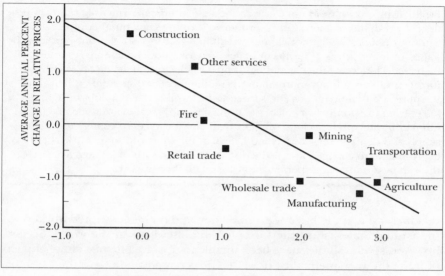

AVERAGE ANNUAL PERCENT CHANGE IN PRODUCTIVITY

Note: FIRE = finance, insurance, and real estate.

Source: Department of Commerce.

BOX 2 **CONSEQUENCES OF PRODUCTIVITY GROWTH**

Rising productivity has been shown to have a variety of beneficial effects:

☐ *The prices of goods produced by industries that have had rapid productivity growth have fallen relative to those of goods from industries with slower productivity growth.* Chart 3 shows average productivity growth and price changes by industry for the 1950–90 period.

☐ *Periods of rapid productivity growth have been accompanied by increases in real wages.* The prices of products in industries experiencing productivity growth also decline relative to wages. This decline in product prices means that real wages tend to rise during periods of rapid productivity growth.

☐ *Periods of rapid productivity growth have also been periods of low inflation.* Productivity growth allows nominal wages to increase without putting pressure on prices.

☐ *Periods of rapid productivity growth have not been associated with large increases in unemployment.* In periods when productivity growth was more rapid, such as the 1960s, unemployment rates have tended to be low. In contrast, periods with slow rates of productivity growth, such as the 1970s, have been periods of relatively high unemployment.

BOX 3   **WHY PRODUCTIVITY GROWTH DOES NOT CAUSE UNEMPLOYMENT**

Productivity growth need not cause an increase in unemployment because, as productivity rises, more goods can be produced with the same number of workers. This means a cost saving, which must result in either increased profits, increased wages, or lower prices. If profits or wages increase, those benefiting from the increase will increase their spending. If prices fall, consumers' incomes will go further and they will buy more. In any case, the increased spending will lead to the purchase of more goods and services, which will create new jobs offsetting losses from the productivity increase. If the new jobs created are not equal in number to the jobs lost, there will be a tendency for wages to change to equate supply and demand for labor. Nonetheless, in the short run some workers are likely to have to change jobs. As the discussion of the costs of job loss makes clear, this can be a traumatic experience for the established worker.

that increasing trade has undermined demand for less-educated workers in the United States, since they are plentiful elsewhere in the world. So far, however, several studies have been unable to discern any substantial impact of trade on wage inequality, however. If increased trade were the cause of growing wage inequality, the relative prices of goods that use highly educated labor would be rising relative to those of goods that use less highly educated labor. But studies have found no evidence of such a change in relative prices. Similarly, if increased trade were responsible for increased wage inequality, the growth of wage differentials would lead firms in all sectors to substitute less-educated labor for more-educated labor. Instead, studies find that virtually all manufacturing industries have increased their relative use of educated labor despite growing wage differentials. Rising wage differentials with greater use of educated labor suggest that demand for skilled labor has been rising broadly in the economy. Thus it appears that most of the demand shift toward highly educated workers must have originated domestically.

Since the use of more-educated labor has increased in all industries, a logical explanation of this trend is technical change. For example, one study shows that people who work with personal computers earn a substantial wage premium over those who do not, and that this can account for half of the increasing gap between the wages of college and high school graduates.

Although changes in labor demand induced by changes in the composition of trade do not appear to explain much of the increase in income inequality, the internationalization of the U.S. economy may affect wages in other ways. For example, the threat of increased import competition or of the relocation of a factory to another country may undermine worker bargaining power or cause a decline in the number of workers employed in unionized firms. At this time, no reliable studies have properly quantified how important such effects have been. In addition, there is no guarantee that the future will resemble the past. Trade could become a more important factor in bringing down the wages of less-educated workers in the future. On the other hand, technical change could move in the direction of economizing on educated labor and making better use of less-educated labor.

In addition to rapidly increasing demand for educated labor, two institutional factors seem to have contributed to rising wage inequality: the decline of unions and the erosion of the minimum wage by inflation. In the early 1970s, 27 percent of the work force were union members. By 1990 that fraction had declined to 16 percent, and it has probably fallen further since. Several studies conclude that this decline can account for about 20 percent of the increase in wage inequality.

In 1970 the minimum wage was 50 percent of the average hourly wage of private production and nonsupervisory workers. By 1992 it had fallen to 40 percent of the average. This erosion of the minimum wage has allowed a substantial fattening of the lower tail of the wage distribution and contributed to increasing wage inequality. The effect of the minimum wage on the distribution of income is less obvious, since it is possible that the decline in the inflation-adjusted minimum wage may have caused an increase in employment of low-wage workers.

Immigration has increased the relative supply of less-educated labor and appears to have contributed to the increasing inequality of income, but the effect has been small. A study of the effects of immigration between 1980 and 1988 found that it explains less than 1 percent of the change in the college–high school wage differential. Although immigration flows were considerably larger in the late 1980s than the early 1980s, this study makes it seem unlikely that immigration could explain more than a few percent of the total change in this differential.

Income Mobility and Economic Opportunity*

Chris Frenze

JOINT ECONOMIC COMMITTEE OF CONGRESS: REPUBLICAN VIEWS

Great attention has been given to changes over time in the average incomes of "quintiles," families or households ranked top to bottom by income and divided into fifths. However, such time-line comparisons between rich and poor ignore a central element of the U.S. economy, which is the extent to which individuals move from one quintile to another. Figures on income mobility are more characteristic of the nature of our fluid society than comparisons of average incomes by quintile, which would only be statistically meaningful if America were a caste society where the people comprising the quintiles remained constant over time.

Unfortunately, while data on average income by quintile has been plentiful, however misleading, data on income mobility has been scarce.

This section, an analysis of data based on income tax returns filed from 1979 through 1988, which were tabulated by the U.S. Department of the Treasury, provides new insights. The Treasury sample consists of 14,351 taxpayers filing returns in all of the above years. This sample tends to understate income mobility to the extent the movement of younger and older filers in and out of the population of taxpayers is missed by the requirement that returns be filed in all years. On the other hand, this understate-

*Joint Economic Committee of Congress, *1993 Joint Economic Report,* April 1, 1993.

ment is at least somewhat offset at the low end of the income scale by the presence of an underclass which does not file tax returns year after year. For our purposes, the bottom quintile consists of those who earn enough income to at least file income tax returns, if not to actually pay taxes.

Earlier studies of income mobility have demonstrated a startling degree of income mobility in as short a period as one year. However, as a January 1992 study noted,[1] additional data over more extended periods were needed to draw more precise conclusions about income mobility over the longer term. This need has now been largely satisfied by the provision of longitudinal panel data from tax return files. However, much more data and research on income dynamics in coming years is needed.

LEVEL OF INCOME MOBILITY BY QUINTILE

The tax return data support the conclusion that the degree of income mobility in American society renders the comparison of quintile income levels over time virtually meaningless. According to the tax data, 85.8 percent of filers in the bottom quintile in 1979 had exited this quintile by 1988. The corresponding mobility rates were 71 percent for the second lowest quintile, 67 percent for the middle quintile, 62.5 percent for the fourth quintile, and 35.3 percent for the top quintile.

Of those in the much discussed top 1 percent, over half, or 52.7 percent, were gone by 1988. These data understate income mobility in the top 1 percent to the extent mortality contributes to mobility and the diffusion of income. Chart 1 displays the income mobility of the various groups.

In all but the top quintile, at least 60 percent of filers exited their 1979 income quintile by 1988, with two-thirds or more exiting in the bottom three quintiles. Though much more stability was observed in the top fifth, over one-third had slipped downward to be replaced by others moving up. Even most of the top 1 percent had exited by 1988, to be replaced by others.

The very high degree of income mobility displayed above shows that the composition of the various quintiles changes greatly over time. A majority of filers have indeed moved to different quintiles between 1979 and 1988. Thus intertemporal comparisons of average wages, earnings, or private incomes of quintiles cannot provide meaningful measures of changes in the income of actual families and persons only temporarily in a given quintile or percentile. Quintiles may be a convenient way of presenting snapshots of income data for a group of people at a certain point in time. Nonethe-

---

[1]JEC/GOP staff study, "Income Mobility and the U.S. Economy: Open Society or Caste System?" released by Congressman Dick Armey, January 1992.

CHART 1   Proportion Moving to Different Quintiles or from Top Percentile, 1979–88

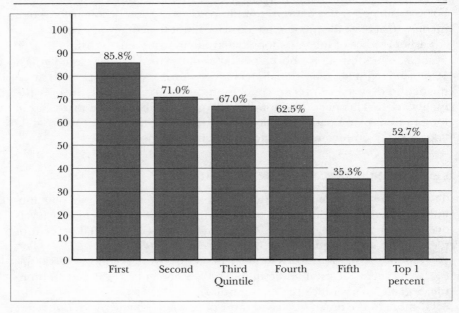

Source: United States Treasury.

less, the notion of a quintile as a fixed economic class or social reality is a statistical mirage.

DIRECTION OF INCOME MOBILITY

Movement is important, but the direction of that movement is more important. While a strong argument can be made for a flexible and open market economy which presents opportunities to lower and middle income workers, instability alone is not necessarily a virtue. [Table 1] summarizes the income mobility data to display the direction of movement between 1979 and 1988. For example, in the third, or middle 1979 fifth, 47.3 percent had moved to a higher quintile by 1988, while 33.0 remained in this same quintile, and 19.7 percent fell into a lower quintile.

Given the relative starting position, the very high mobility from the bottom quintile obviously reflects improvement. In addition, the upward movement in the second, third, and fourth quintiles is much larger than

TABLE 1   America on the Move

1979 QUINTILE	PERCENT IN QUINTILE IN 1979	PERCENT IN EACH QUINTILE IN 1988				
		1ST	2ND	3RD	4TH	5TH
1st	100%	14.2%	20.7%	25.0%	25.3%	14.7%
2nd	100	10.9	29.0	29.6	19.5	11.1
3rd	100	5.7	14.0	33.0	32.3	15.0
4th	100	3.1	9.3	14.8	37.5	35.4
5th	100	1.1	4.4	9.4	20.3	64.7

Source: United States Treasury.

downward movement. For example, 60 percent of the second quintile had moved to one of the higher three quintiles by 1988. Over this same time, only 10.9 percent had fallen from the second into the lowest quintile.

In the long-overdue debate over the significance of income mobility, some may argue that mobility would tend to reflect slippage, especially among the middle class. The data contradict this contention. Of those in the middle quintile in 1979, nearly half moved upward to the fourth or fifth quintiles by 1988. Overall, in the bottom four quintiles, net improvement was the rule, not the exception.

DETAIL ON INCOME MOBILITY, 1979–88

Table 1 displays the movement of filers from 1979 quintiles to their positions in 1988. Each row can be read across: of 100 percent of each 1979 quintile, the table shows their dispersion among the various fifths by 1988.

About 86 percent of those in the bottom quintile in 1979 had managed to raise their incomes by 1988 enough to have moved up to a higher quintile. The data show that these were not all grouped at the bottom at the second quintile. While 20.7 percent were in the second quintile, 25.0 percent had made it into the middle fifth, and another 25.3 percent into the second highest quintile. The 14.7 percent in the top quintile was actually higher than the 14.2 percent still stuck in the bottom fifth.

In other words, a member of the bottom income bracket in 1979 would have a better chance of moving to the top income bracket by 1988 than remaining in the bottom bracket.

In the second quintile, 71 percent had exited between 1979 and 1988. Though 29.0 percent still remained in the second quintile in 1988, 29.6

percent had moved up to the third quintile, 19.5 percent to the fourth, and 11.1 percent to the top quintile. Only 10.9 percent had moved down to the lowest quintile.

Of those in the middle quintile in 1979, 32.3 percent had moved to the fourth quintile and 15.0 percent to the fifth quintile by 1988.

Over this period, 47.3 percent had moved up, while 19.7 percent had moved down. The net effect of income mobility in the middle range clearly reflected net overall improvement.

While the fourth quintile exhibited powerful income mobility, the top quintile is the most stable. However, all income mobility from the top quintile is by definition downward mobility. The share of this group dropping into lower quintiles was 35.3 percent, while 27.2 percent of the fourth quintile also dropped at least one quintile. Many of these with declining fortunes are still better off than many of those with upward mobility from a low quintile, however, the overall pattern is that there tends to be strong upward mobility from the lower quintiles, while income mobility from a high level often reflects economic reversals. Without income mobility, many in the top fifth would be better off, and the great majority of those in the lower quintiles would be worse off. Income mobility reflects improvement in the lower four quintiles, but this fact has been virtually ignored in public discussion of income trends.

While 35.3 percent fell from the top quintile into the fourth quintile or below, 40.0 percent of the bottom quintile had moved into the fourth or fifth quintiles by 1988. Of all of those in the bottom quintile in 1979, about two-thirds, or 65 percent, had moved to the middle or higher quintiles by 1988. These data demonstrate that the U.S. economy, not without problems over this period, still remains dynamic, open, and productive enough to permit most Americans in the bottom three-fifths to work their way up the economic ladder. What is needed are policies to ensure that this flexibility and opportunity are extended as widely as possible, especially to those who actually fall below the bottom fifth of taxpayers.

Currently there are two models of the American economy, one static, and the other dynamic. The first portrays the United States as a caste system and misapplies the characteristics of a permanent income strata to those only temporarily moving through income brackets. The alternative view portrays a much more complex and interesting social reality in which the composition of income classes are in constant flux. According to this latter point of view, simplistic generalizations about actual persons and families (or "the rich" and "the poor") cannot be drawn from data on a conceptual artifice that does not exist as such in reality.

The empirical data support the view of the market economy as a dynamic and open society that provides opportunity to those who participate. There is no evidence of stagnation, with the turnover rate in the most stable quintile—the top fifth—exceeding 35 percent. The turnover rates in the bottom four quintiles were at least 60 percent over the period, with most of this reflecting upward progress. Analysis that assumes or suggests stable composition of family or household income quintiles rests on invalid assumptions.

It makes no sense to draw sweeping conclusions such as "the income of the bottom 20 percent of families fell" in a 15-year period when most of the people originally in that category have long since improved their standard of living enough to have moved up from the bracket entirely.

Soaking the Rich*

ROBERT BARRO

The 1993 changes in the U.S. tax law focused on increases in marginal income tax rates on the "rich." The extra revenues that were thought to derive from these higher rates underlay the administration's contention that its fiscal package was an equal mix of spending cuts and tax increases. A key issue, however, is whether the increases in marginal tax rates at the top will raise any revenue at all. The history of responses to tax rate changes from 1981 to 1991 suggests that the receipts generated will probably be close to zero and may well be negative. The reason is that upper-income people are very responsive to changes in the tax code; when tax rates rise, the reported amount of taxable income drops sharply.

Neither the Democrats nor the Republicans wanted to make this argument in 1993. The Democrats, of course, did not want to acknowledge that higher tax rates on the rich would generate little revenue. The Republicans did not want to press the point because, first, they did not want to look like the advocates of the rich, and, second, if tax receipts did not rise, then they could not argue that the Democrats had raised taxes. One would have

*This is an excerpt from Robert Barro, *Getting It Right* (Cambridge, Mass.: MIT Press, 1996). Dr. Dan Feenberg of the National Bureau of Economic Research assisted with this material. Robert Barro is professor of economics at Harvard University.

thought, however, that an increase in tax rates that produced no revenue was a good deal worse than one that generated lots of revenue.

Chart 1 shows for 1960–1991 the fraction of total federal income taxes paid by the upper 0.5 percent of the income distribution (returns with adjusted gross incomes above about $220,000 in 1991). The most relevant experience for evaluating the 1993 tax change is the period of changing tax policy from 1981 to 1991.

For the top 0.5 percent of the income distribution, the most important changes are the shifts in the marginal tax rates at high incomes. The period 1981–1991 featured a cut in the top marginal rate on unearned income from 70 percent to 50 percent in the 1981 law, a cut in the top rate on all forms of income to 28 percent in the 1986 law (except that this law raised the rate on long-term capital gains), and an increase in the top rate to 31 percent (or, more accurately, a couple of percentage points higher because of phase-out provisions for deductions) in the 1990 law.

The first observation from Chart 1 is that the increase in the reported taxable incomes of the rich after the 1981 law was so great that the share of taxes paid by this group rose from 14 percent in 1981 to 18 percent in 1984–1985, despite (or rather because of) the reduction in the top mar-

CHART 1 Share of Income Tax Paid by Top 0.5 Percent of the Income Distribution.

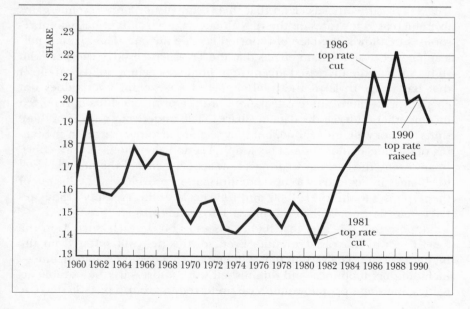

ginal tax rate. The much-ridiculed Laffer curve—the idea that lower tax rates could generate more revenue—worked brilliantly at upper incomes, even if not for the overall economy.

The share of the rich in taxes paid for 1986—21 percent—is inflated by the surge in capital gains realizations in anticipation of the rise in the capital gains tax rate in 1987. But the principal observation about the 1986 reform is that the share paid by this group remained nearly constant—between 20 and 22 percent—from 1986 to 1990, despite the sharp cut in the top marginal tax rate on most forms of income. In particular, in 1988, the final year of the Reagan administration—and, in that sense, the pinnacle of the "greedy 1980s"—the share of the rich reached its peak of 22 percent. (I do not know whether one-fifth is a "fair share" for the top 0.5 percent of income recipients to pay, but it does mean that the average person in this group pays forty times as much in federal income taxes as the typical person.)

More information came from the rise in the top marginal tax rate in the 1990 law. This change was followed by a *decline* in the fraction of taxes paid by the rich from 20 percent in 1990 to 19 percent in 1991. Thus, the pattern in which changes in the top tax rates cause a dramatic response in the opposite direction of reported taxable incomes works for tax rate increases as well as for tax rate decreases. This finding is especially noteworthy because the 1993 income tax changes were basically more of the same that was contained in the 1990 law.

U.S. Treasury officials claim that their estimates of large revenue gains from increased tax rates on the rich already take account of behavioral responses that lower the base of reported taxable income. This claim is misleading, because the main effects that the Treasury considers are portfolio shifts, such as the increased incentive to hold tax-exempt bonds (an effect that has to be trivial if the total supply of tax-exempt bonds does not change). Left out of these calculations are the principal shifts in reported incomes that underlie the data in Chart 1. The underlying sources of these shifts are not well understood, but they seem to involve changes in the timing of income, exploitation of tax loopholes, and alterations in work effort. In any event, the best way to project how tax payments by the rich will react to changes in tax rates is to use the information provided by the history of the responses to the 1981, 1986, and 1990 tax laws; the Treasury's estimates fail to take account of the clear message from this history.

Suppose that it is true that higher tax rates on the rich, such as in the 1993 law, will not raise revenue. Even so, the rich will suffer from the higher tax rates. The various methods employed to lower taxable income—including tax loopholes and diminished work effort—are undesirable activities that these people would have preferred to avoid. Thus, the income tax proposals will succeed in burdening the rich even if they fail to generate revenue. . . .

To me it is obvious that a tax rate hike that makes one group suffer—even the rich—but provides no revenue is bad economic policy. Since I do not trust my instincts, however, I surveyed some of my left-wing friends and relatives: I asked, What do you think of a policy that makes the rich worse off but produces no revenue and therefore provides no direct benefits for the nonrich? Remarkably, the results were mixed. Some respondents would be willing to give up resources to reduce the incomes of the rich, so that some measures of income inequality would narrow. Apparently some people view the presence of wealthy people as similar to environmental pollution. One can only hope that this class-warfare mentality is not the driving force behind most policy decisions in Washington.

QUESTIONS FOR ANALYSIS

1. What are the effects of productivity growth? Does productivity growth have to cause unemployment? Why or why not?

2. Are there any reasons why we should be concerned about increases or decreases in income inequality? If so, what are they?

3. According to President Clinton's Council of Economic Advisers, "Stagnant wages and slow total compensation growth since the early 1970s largely reflect a substantial slowdown in productivity growth." Why would a slowdown in productivity growth be expected to have this effect? Explain.

4. President Clinton's Council of Economic Advisers concludes that: "Rising wage differentials with greater use of educated labor suggest that demand for skilled labor has been rising broadly in the economy." Can you show that this is the case, using demand and supply curves for educated labor?

5. Other factors cited by President Clinton's Council of Economic Advisers as possible reasons for growing wage inequality are "the decline of unions and the erosion of the minimum wage by inflation." Are increases in *wage* inequality the same thing as increases in *income* inequality? Why or why not? Is it possible that a big hike in the minimum wage might raise, not lower, income inequality? Why or why not?

6. According to the Republican members of Congress's Joint Economic Committee, "Great attention has been given to changes over time in the average incomes of 'quintiles,' families or households ranked top to bottom by income and divided into fifths. However, such time-line comparisons between rich and poor ignore a central element of the U.S. economy, which is the extent to which individuals move from one quintile to another." Do you agree that such movement is important? Why or why not?

7. The Republican members of the Joint Economic Committee state that: "The empirical data support the view of the market economy as a dynamic and open society that provides opportunity to those who participate." Do you agree? Why or why not?

8. Do you agree with the following conclusion: "It makes no sense to draw sweeping conclusions such as 'the income of the bottom 20 percent of families fell' in a 15-year period when most of the people originally in that category have long since improved their standard of living enough to have moved up from the bracket entirely." Why do you agree or disagree?

9. According to Robert Barro, "a tax rate hike that makes one group suffer—even the rich—but provides no revenue is bad economic policy." Do you agree? Why or why not?

10. Why, according to Professor Barro, will the rich suffer from higher tax rates even if higher tax rates on the rich do not raise revenue?

PART FOUR

COMPETITION AND ANTITRUST POLICY

Competition is a major characteristic of the United States economy. The first article, which appeared in the *Philadelphia Inquirer,* describes changes in the market for natural gas, as competition becomes more important there. The second article, also from the *Inquirer,* describes Microsoft's efforts to utilize the World Wide Web. In the third article, the Antitrust Division describes eight recent antitrust cases.

Competition in the Natural Gas Market*

PHILADELPHIA INQUIRER

If you've been chilled by this winter's bills for natural-gas heating, take heart: The long-term outlook for gas prices seems considerably more springlike.

The reason is that retail competition appears to be coming, slowly but surely, to residential gas customers.

Commercial and industrial customers already are allowed to choose their gas suppliers in both Pennsylvania and New Jersey. Some residential users are getting that same option under pilot programs in both states, with PSE&G [Public Service Electric & Gas] customers in Pennsauken expected to be among the first guinea pigs.

And supporters of the recent push for retail electrical competition in Pennsylvania are gearing up to push for natural-gas competition, too.

"We support natural-gas competition," Tim Reeves, a spokesman for Gov. Ridge, said yesterday. He said the governor was "quietly working" with the chairman of the Public Utility Commission, John M. Quain, and legislators to reach an "agreeable proposal" for retail competition.

One of those legislators, Rep. Frank Tulli Jr. (R. Hershey), has been circulating a draft of a bill that he plans to introduce in March.

*This article appeared in the *Philadelphia Inquirer* on February 28, 1997. The author is Jeff Gelles.

"We'd like to make Pennsylvania the first state to have natural-gas competition for all three classes of service—residential, commercial and industrial," Tulli said yesterday.

The last two winters' weather may prove an unexpected ally to Tulli and other advocates of retail gas competition, who argue that market forces will drive down the prices paid by consumers.

The severe cold a year ago kept wholesale prices high all summer, when utilities were trying to restock their supplies. Then came November's unusual cold snap. Gas utilities raised their prices to historical highs—and then helped bid up the price of gas futures, fearing the worst from the rest of the winter.

At the market's peak, gas futures rose to $4.50 per 1,000 cubic feet in mid-December for January deliveries, a level not seen since the early 1980s, when utility customers were more insulated from price fluctuations.

This time, because of the influences of price deregulation throughout the energy business, gas customers were less protected.

Area utilities raised their gas prices by 8 to 12 percent in the fall, and they haven't completely stopped.

"This was the sharpest run-up that the ratepayers of gas utilities have seen, period," said Richard W. LeLash, a Connecticut consultant on utility issues.

That was the bad news. The good news, say many inside and outside the gas industry, is in the long-term outlook:

☐ Prices dropped as swiftly as they rose. The price for March deliveries, which peaked at $3.40 per 1,000 cubic feet in December, had dropped to $1.78 by the time bidding closed on Monday.

☐ Wellhead prices generally—the wholesale price paid for gas as it comes out of the ground—have been remarkably stable for the last 10 years. That stability is usually attributed to advances in technology and increased exploration spurred by decontrol of the market beginning during the natural-gas-supply crisis of the late 1970s.

☐ Competition among suppliers of gas to industrial and commercial customers has shown signs of success where it has been tried.

Whatever the causes, the natural-gas market appears to be changing dramatically. In the space of just one year, for example, the federal Energy Information Administration dropped its projection of the cost of natural gas in 2015 by almost 20 percent, from $2.63 to $2.15 per 1,000 cubic feet, in 1995 dollars.

"Those of us in the energy field believe that there are not really long-term price increases coming, other than what you expect from inflation," said Jay Hakes, who heads the Energy Department agency. ". . . The last two years that we have the data, for '94 and '95, there were more reserves added to the system than there was gas consumed."

So far, competition among producers has had limited effect on what residential customers pay, because the rest of the business—interstate pipeline companies and local utilities—remain regulated by the federal and state governments.

"The people who have benefited the most from it are the big customers, like the electrical utilities, that have the ability to buy in bulk," Hakes said.

In Pennsylvania, the rule is that customers who want to choose their own supplier must purchase more than 5 million cubic feet of gas a year, or be part of a buying group of no more than 10 customers that purchase that much together.

A typical residential customer uses 100,000 to 150,000 cubic feet a year, said PUC Commissioner John Hanger.

Hanger said competition in gas would benefit customers much as he expects it to in electricity, though he said the savings would be smaller because gas costs do not vary as widely as electricity costs. He said about half of Pennsylvania residents use gas for home heating, and pay about $6 to $9 per 1,000 cubic feet.

"The savings numbers we are looking at are probably in the 10 to 15 percent range for an average customer," Hanger said, adding that the benefits of any move away from a monopoly-controlled marketplace were tough to predict.

That is about how much business customers in New Jersey have saved since 1994, when the market was opened, said Wendy Kaczerski, a spokeswoman for the state's Board of Public Utilities.

PSE&G officials are more reserved in their attitude toward residential choice, but say they are confident that they can compete.

"PSE&G is the biggest purchaser of natural gas in the state of New Jersey. So how much more someone will be able to beat our price is something that we'll learn. It may be difficult," said spokesman Paul Rosengren.

Commercial and industrial choice has not been entirely to PSE&G's liking. The company has lost about 10,000 business customers—representing about half of commercial and industrial gas consumption—since supplier-competition began, said spokesman George R. Koodray.

Koodray said the customers were lured away largely by a tax advantage enjoyed by third-party suppliers. He said PSE&G supported choice, "provided that choice comes about in an environment that sets a level playing field."

Supporters of gas competition say it should be easier to achieve than telephone or electrical competition for one key reason: Unlike electrical and phone utilities, gas utilities generally do not produce what they sell. They are largely middlemen and deliverers, albeit with complex and expensive delivery systems.

So-called "stranded investment"—typified by Peco's concern that customers, not stockholders, should bear the cost of investments made with regulatory approval, such as the Limerick nuclear power plant—is much less of a problem in the gas business.

Technical hurdles are not insignificant. The biggest: Unlike some businesses, residences need a guarantee of uninterrupted service.

It is unclear whether and how gas competition might affect customers of the municipally owned Philadelphia Gas Works, which serves about 500,000 city customers and is not regulated by the state.

Chris Kimmerle, executive director of the Philadelphia Gas Commission, which regulates PGW, said its high rate of unpaid accounts posed a particular problem. "The fear is that to the extent that you let the marketers come into the market, they will cherry-pick the best customers and leave the worst customers for the utility," Kimmerle said.

Microsoft and the Internet*

PHILADELPHIA INQUIRER

Airline tickets, hotel reservations, books, cars, CDs, stocks. You can use a computer to buy them all on the World Wide Web with just a few clicks of a mouse and a charge-card number.

And when you do, chances are you will find a familiar company in an unfamiliar role: Microsoft Corp.

A little more than a year ago, the notion that Microsoft would be running a car-buying service or a travel agency over the Internet would have been considered far-fetched if not laughable. A late bloomer on the Net, the Redmond, Wash., software producer whose Windows operating systems run on 80 percent to 90 percent of the world's personal computers, was still trying to find its way among the wired set. There was talk that Microsoft was too big, too slow and too set in its ways to "get the Net," to be a player in what was considered the next frontier of personal computing.

Today, all that has changed. More than 20,000 Microsoft workers worldwide, from chairman Bill Gates on down, have embraced the Internet like a long-lost child.

"A year ago, when you said Internet, most people tended to think of Netscape," said Brad Chase, a long-time systems strategist for Microsoft, refer-

*This article appeared in the *Philadelphia Inquirer* on March 23, 1997. The authors are Paul Andrews and Michele Matassa Flores.

ring to the Silicon Valley company whose World Wide Web browser popularized Web surfing for millions. "Today, when you say Internet, most people tend to think of Microsoft as well."

Part of the credit goes to the Microsoft marketing and deal-making machine. The company and its indefatigable chairman seem to be everywhere, from magazine covers and TV newscasts to Web ads and stadium billboards. Gates has been photographed golfing with President Clinton, meeting with astronauts, sharing a laugh with Tom Brokaw, and playing bridge with Warren Buffett.

"The Internet is a part of everything we do at Microsoft," Gates said in a recent New York appearance.

So sweeping has the transformation been, in so brief a period of time, that some fear Microsoft is gaining too much power too fast. If the Internet becomes the medium of choice for global communications, business transactions, reading the news or buying a car, consolidating the Net's capabilities in the hands of a single company raises troublesome issues of information and cultural control.

Could Gates & Co. really dominate a mechanism as vast as the Web the way Microsoft dominates desktop software? Gates himself has called the idea impossible. Yet Microsoft continues to enter new Web arenas with more resources, business savvy and aggressiveness than any of its rivals.

With more than $9 billion cash, Microsoft can buy or partner its way into virtually any technology it wants. As a result, the Microsoft hand can be seen at work in just about every strategic Internet technology: news, entertainment, financial transactions, e-mail, databases and communications.

Perhaps the biggest new mantra at Microsoft is "content." The Microsoft Network, Microsoft's online service, provides an entry onto the Web for two million users and may pass CompuServe as the No. 2 provider behind America Online this year. MSNBC, a news venture with NBC, delivers news to Web users.

Besides CarPoint, Microsoft's Internet car-buying guide, the company has inaugurated or will soon introduce a host of other media services including Expedia, a consumer travel agency; Mungo Park, an adventure travel site; Underwire, a hip site for young women; Slate, a political journal edited by East Coast media insider Michael Kinsley; Mint, an MTV-like electronic 'zine (magazine); and Sidewalk, a city-based arts-and-entertainment guide. Besides Expedia, Microsoft is developing a business-travel site under a two-year exclusive arrangement with American Express, the biggest travel agent in the world.

Microsoft also is exerting its influence on the "back end" of the Internet, the computers that ferry data around the Net. Called "servers," they increasingly feature Microsoft's high-end Windows NT software for building and maintaining data and services on Web sites. A sluggish seller when it was first released three years ago, NT has exploded in recent months, nearly tripling last year's sales in markets throughout the world.

Microsoft is making software for managing Web sites, for managing databases, for handling electronic commerce and financial transactions on the Web, and for building intranets, those Web-like networks that corporations and businesses are using to streamline in-house handling of forms, company announcements, electronic mail, etc. By 2000, intranets are expected to generate $10 billion to $30 billion worth of business.

Microsoft is hardly alone in its initiatives. IBM, Apple, Netscape, Sun Microsystems and others promote their products in similar ways. But no other single company has as sweeping a presence on the Web as Microsoft, which is one reason some expect the federal government will ultimately step in.

Last summer, O'Reilly & Associates, a pioneering Web-server maker in Sebastopol, Calif., filed a complaint about Microsoft's pricing policies on Windows NT server, calling them anti-competitive.

Netscape, whose Navigator browser has led the market since the Web first exploded in 1995, chimed in with allegations of its own regarding browser and server pricing. After Netscape hired aggressive antitrust attorney Gary Reback, the Justice Department reopened an investigation into Microsoft's business practices that began in 1995.

Justice Department officials have consistently refused to talk about the scope of the inquiry. Netscape has nearly completed responding to inquiries, Reback said. Meanwhile, Texas' attorney general has requested documents from Microsoft regarding possible restraint of trade. Other states have contacted Texas officials to discuss the inquiry. Microsoft said it is cooperating but does not yet know the specific subject of the action.

If past experience holds, the investigations are unlikely to have much impact on the way Microsoft does business. In July 1994, Microsoft signed consent orders with the Justice Department and the European Commission to end pricing practices on its Windows and DOS software that put competitors at a disadvantage in selling to computer manufacturers. But by that time, Windows was already the operating system of choice, and Microsoft's market share has increased since the decision.

Although catalyzed by an often-cited Gates speech on Pearl Harbor Day, Dec. 7, 1995, Microsoft's Internet development extends back to 1991, when it registered the "microsoft.com" name, giving the company an official Internet address. Prodded by memos from junior executives, Gates and the Microsoft hierarchy kept tabs on the Net while withholding any major commitment of resources.

Starting last summer, though, the shift entered warp speed:

□ In August, Microsoft released an upgraded version of Internet Explorer, which has boosted the company's browser market share from the 4-percent-to-6-percent range to 17 percent or higher.

□ In September, Microsoft issued an upgrade of Windows NT—to 4.0—accelerating its use in corporations and large enterprises.

□ In November, Microsoft came out with its Merchant Server, a product for shopping on the Net, and a new version of Microsoft Front Page for designing and managing home pages and Web sites.

□ In December, Microsoft upgraded its Microsoft Network with a TV-like look and a number of new features.

□ At the Internet World conference in New York in December, Microsoft announced the acquisition of NetCarta, a Scotts Valley, Calif., maker of Web-site management products, and a strategic partnership with PointCast, a Santa Clara, Calif., Web company that pioneered "push" technology for broadcasting online information to users' computer screens instead of their having to surf for it.

□ Expected by summer is yet another upgrade of Internet Explorer, version 4.0, featuring "push" technology.

Microsoft's dominance, or even success, on the Web is far from guaranteed. The company anticipates losing substantial sums on the Web, an estimated $300 million to $400 million a year for three years, before it starts to turn a profit, according to No. 2 in command Steve Ballmer. Although interactive media have generated $950 million in revenue already, it will be three to four years before his division sees black ink, said John Neilson, chief of Microsoft's interactive-service media division.

Microsoft's ability to dominate categories it targets may be behind a backlash movement in Silicon Valley dubbed Anyone But Microsoft. Stephen Auditore, the founder of Zona Research, an industry analyst in Redwood City, Calif., defines ABM as the willingness of some companies to do business with anyone but Microsoft no matter how much money it costs them in the long run. Auditore has characterized the battle between Silicon Valley and Microsoft as a *jihad,* or holy war.

The valley's big hope is Java, a programming language that can be used to produce software that does not need Microsoft's Windows. Microsoft rivals say Java will become popular on new computer devices ranging from simple Internet appliances to hand-held computers. IBM has more than 1,000 programmers working on Java applications for business and finance.

Sun Microsystems, which created Java; Oracle, a leading database manufacturer; Netscape; and countless Web start-up companies are creating new software in Java as well. Prominent venture capitalist John Doerr compared Java to a drug that "makes programmers go crazy when you rub it on them."

Skeptics question whether Java will dent Microsoft, however. They note that Microsoft licensed the technology from Sun a year ago and since has offered its own form of improved Java designed to keep the Microsoft name and Windows prominent in Java applications. Web analyst Jesse Berst, host of a popular industry-news Web site anchordesk.com, said Microsoft is in the process of "kidnapping" Java.

What's Microsoft's secret? Neilson ticks off a litany of successful strategies: Hire smart people; empower them with "small company" ownership of projects; constantly second-guess mistakes, asking what was learned to avoid repeating; and, above all, pay attention to customers. When all else fails, purchase or outspend the competition.

It's a textbook formula for success, though, and countless companies dominant in their markets or otherwise have followed it without matching Microsoft's inexorable growth. Isn't there an X factor that puts Microsoft in a league all its own?

"I think it's definitely that we're more relentless," said Neilson. "We have people here who hate to lose."

Eight Recent Antitrust Cases*

ANTITRUST DIVISION, U.S. DEPARTMENT OF JUSTICE

ONE: THERMAL FAX PAPER

After a two year investigation coordinated with Canadian antitrust officials, the Division and its Canadian counterpart in July 1994 brought criminal charges under their respective laws against an international cartel that had fixed prices in the $120 million a year thermal fax paper market. The Division's criminal information charged a Japanese corporation, two U.S. subsidiaries of Japanese firms and an executive of one of the firms with conspiring to charge higher prices to thermal fax paper customers in North America. Thermal fax paper is used primarily by small businesses and home fax machine owners. The defendants pleaded guilty and agreed to pay $6.4 million in fines.

The Division and Canadian officials are continuing the joint investigation into the fax paper industry under the U.S.-Canada Mutual Legal Assistance Treaty. This case was the Division's first criminal prosecution of a major Japanese corporation headquartered in Tokyo as well as the first to be coordinated with Canadian authorities, and illustrates the type of international antitrust cooperation that will occur more frequently in the future.

*This includes excerpts from the *Antitrust Division Annual Report for Fiscal Year 1994* (Washington, D.C.: Government Printing Office, 1995).

TWO: INDUSTRIAL DIAMONDS

In February 1994, the Division obtained an indictment of General Electric, DeBeers Centenary and two individuals charging them with conspiring to raise list prices in the $500 million a year industrial diamond industry. The two corporate defendants account for 80 percent of the industrial diamond market and allegedly fixed prices by secretly exchanging information about intended price hikes. The price increases went into effect worldwide in February and March of 1992. DeBeers and the two individuals remained overseas and beyond the reach of the U.S. courts. Trial of General Electric began in October 1994, but charges were dismissed after the presentation of the Government's case. The Division remains committed to aggressive criminal antitrust enforcement against international price-fixing cartels that raise prices to consumers and businesses in the United States.

THREE: GLASS MANUFACTURING TECHNOLOGY

In a major case designed to remove anticompetitive restraints imposed on American exports, the Division in May 1994 charged Pilkington, a British firm, and its U.S. subsidiary with monopolizing the flat glass market. The complaint alleged that Pilkington, which dominates the $15 billion a year international flat glass industry, foreclosed U.S. firms from foreign markets. Flat glass is used for windows and architectural panels by the construction industry and for windshields and windows by the automobile industry.

The Complaint alleged that Pilkington entered into unreasonably restrictive licensing arrangements with its most likely competitors, then over the course of almost three decades used these arrangements and threats of litigation to prevent American firms from competing to design, build and operate flat glass plants in other countries. By the time the Division filed its Complaint, Pilkington's patents had long since expired and its technology was in the public domain. A Consent Decree accepted by Pilkington to settle the case will bar it from restraining American and foreign firms who desire to sell their technology outside the United States. As a result, American firms will be able to compete for the 50 new glass plants expected to be built around the world over the next six years, resulting in an estimated increase in U.S. export revenues of as much as $1.25 billion during that period. This enforcement action builds on the Bush Administration's 1992 announcement that it would challenge such conduct and illustrates the Division's determination to address anticompetitive conduct that prevents

American firms from competing for business on fair terms in international markets.

FOUR: MILK AND DAIRY PRODUCTS CASES

As of September 30, 1994, the Division had filed 124 criminal cases against 73 corporations and 78 individuals in the milk and dairy products industry. To date, 63 corporations and 57 individuals have been convicted, and fines imposed total approximately $59 million. Twenty-seven individuals have been sentenced to serve a total of 4,774 days in jail, or an average of approximately 6 months. Civil damages assessed total approximately $8 million.

This sustained effort has broken up conspiracies that were illegally raising the price of milk supplied to children in public school districts across the country, including federally subsidized school lunch programs, as well as the price of dairy products supplied to the United States military. In FY 94, the division filed 18 criminal cases against 14 corporations and 11 individuals in the milk and dairy products industry. Seventeen grand juries in 14 states continue investigations in this industry.

FIVE: CELLULAR COMMUNICATIONS

In July 1994, the Division challenged the proposed acquisition by AT&T of McCaw Cellular, the nation's largest cellular telephone carrier, because this vertical merger could have raised prices and chilled innovation in cellular telephone services. These competitive concerns were addressed in a Consent Decree under which

□ long-distance rivals of AT&T will have access to McCaw systems equal to AT&T's access;

□ cellular rivals of McCaw that use AT&T equipment will continue to have access to necessary products and will be free of interference from AT&T should they wish to change equipment suppliers; and

□ AT&T and McCaw will not misuse confidential information obtained from AT&T equipment customers or McCaw equipment suppliers.

The Consent Decree allows the parties to seek the potential benefits of integration in cellular services but prevents abuse of their economic power in the cellular services, cellular long distance and telecommunications equipment markets.

SIX: PERSONAL COMPUTER OPERATING SYSTEMS

The Division in July 1994 charged Microsoft, the world's largest computer software company, with violating the antimonopoly provisions of Section 2 of the Sherman Act. Microsoft licensed its MS-DOS and Windows technology on a "per processor" basis that required personal computer manufacturers to pay a fee to Microsoft for each computer shipped, even if the computer did not contain Microsoft's software. Microsoft's dominant position in the market induced many personal computer manufacturers to accept these per processor contracts, which penalized the manufacturers if they dealt with Microsoft's competitors. The Division's Complaint further alleged that Microsoft's licensing contracts bound computer manufacturers to the contracts for an unreasonably long period of time. As a result of these practices, the ability of rival operating systems to compete was impaired, innovation was slowed and consumer choice was limited. Microsoft also imposed overly restrictive nondisclosure agreements on software companies that participated in trial testing of new software, thereby impeding the ability of those firms to work with Microsoft's operating system rivals.

Microsoft agreed to accept a Consent Decree that enjoins these and other restrictive practices, and the Decree was filed along with the Division's Complaint. The tentative settlement was reached in close cooperation with the competition enforcement authorities of the European Commission, which had been investigating Microsoft's conduct since mid-1993, and marked the first coordinated effort of the two enforcement bodies in initiating and settling an antitrust case.

SEVEN: DEPARTMENT OF DEFENSE PROCUREMENT

The division challenged as an unreasonable restraint on competition a "teaming arrangement" between Alliant Techsystems and Aerojet-General to supply the Department of Defense with cluster bombs. The two defendants are the only two U.S. suppliers of cluster bombs, and their agreement not to compete on the DOD contract raised the price of the bombs substantially. The Division negotiated a resolution that recoups $12 million for taxpayers on DOD's 1992 procurement—about a ten percent savings. The case stemmed from coordinated efforts by the Departments of Defense and Justice. The Departments have worked to formalize their cooperation on competition policy in the defense industry based on the recommendations of the Defense Services Board Task Force on Defense Mergers, an interagency working group in which the Division participated . . .

EIGHT: COLLEGES

During the prior Administration, the Division charged that the Ivy League universities and MIT had conspired to fix the prices that financial aid applicants paid to attend those schools. The government alleged that the defendants met regularly to avoid competing against each other in the amount of financial aid—that is, tuition discounts—offered to applicants. The Ivy League schools entered into a Consent Decree that prohibited such agreements. MIT chose to litigate the matter. After a trial in 1992, the district court ruled that MIT had violated the antitrust laws. The Court of Appeals for the Third Circuit subsequently remanded the case for further analysis.

In December 1993, the Division and MIT settled the case when MIT agreed to abide by certain standards of conduct in the future. Those standards allow MIT to agree on general principles for determining financial aid with other colleges that adhere to a need-blind admissions policy and that award students financial aid to meet their full needs. Under the standards, colleges may not agree on the amount or composition of aid offered to individual applicants, on tuition rates or on faculty salaries. In October 1994, Congress enacted legislation that allows colleges following need-blind admissions policies only a more limited form of cooperation on financial aid matters than were set forth in the MIT standards of conduct.

QUESTIONS FOR ANALYSIS

1. Commissioner John Hanger of the Pennsylvania Public Utility Commission estimates that competition in gas may result in 10 to 15 percent savings for consumers. Why?

2. Why is the Justice Department interested in Microsoft's practices?

3. What pricing policies would you regard as "anti-competitive"? Why?

4. According to the Antitrust Division, an international cartel fixed prices in the thermal fax paper market. Why is this against the law?

5. The Antitrust Division challenged as an unreasonable restraint on competition a "teaming arrangement" between Alliant Techsystems and Aerojet-General to supply the Department of Defense with cluster bombs. Why?

PART FIVE

THE

ENVIRONMENT

Many people, including distinguished scientists and leading statesmen and stateswomen, are worried about what is happening to the environment; others feel that economic growth is being curtailed unnecessarily by alarmists who exaggerate the environmental risks. The first article, from the *New York Times* says that, "while green power itself is in retreat, the grass-roots support for it is still widespread." The second article, by President Clinton's Council of Economic Advisers, describes some of the environmental policies of the Clinton administration.

Green Power Wanes, but Not at the Grass Roots*

NEW YORK TIMES

Windmills, solar panels, steam energy from deep in the earth. Many Americans have yearned to produce energy without polluting the air and water or burning irreplaceable fuels like coal, oil and natural gas.

But renewable sources of power have proved to be less than reliable in recent years. They have failed to supply large amounts of energy and, perhaps most important, cannot compete with the cheap power derived from fossil fuels.

For a time in the late 1980's and early 1990's, the promise of unlimited renewable energy seemed close to realization. Consumers, scientists and entrepreneurs were fascinated. And the companies involved in alternative power sources multiplied, while researchers made breakthroughs that lowered costs. Wind energy produced power for about 5 cents a kilowatt hour, nearing the levels produced at huge coal-burning and nuclear plants. Companies like Kenetech Corporation in Livermore, Calif., developed propeller-churning turbines designed to make wind a mainstream source of energy.

*This article appeared in the *New York Times* on March 9, 1997. The author is Agis Salpukas.

STRONG PUBLIC SUPPORT

But in the past five years, the promise of renewable power has become a distant hope. Incentives provided by state regulators and utilities have disappeared. Federal research funds have been cut by a budget-conscious Congress. The industry itself has stumbled. Kenetech's newest turbines were flawed, according to a stockholder lawsuit and some industry analysts, and the company's wind subsidiary was forced to seek bankruptcy protection.

But while green power itself is in retreat, the grass-roots support for it is still widespread. Central and South West Corporation, an electric and natural gas utility in the Southwest, recently held town meetings with some of its 1.7 million customers and found strong support for alternative energy sources. Most residents said they were willing to pay from $5 to $7 more a month to have solar or other alternatives supply part of their energy.

CHART 1   Total Domestic Production of Energy from Geothermal, Wind, Waste, Wood, Photovoltaic and Solar Thermal Sources

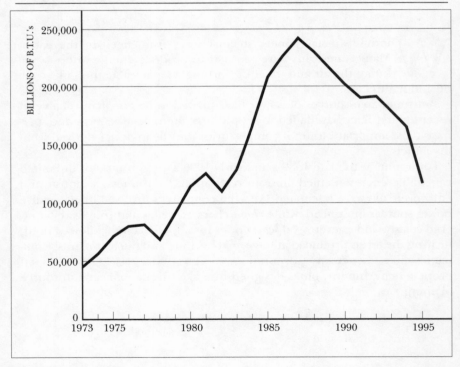

Source: Department of Energy.

"There is a market out there for renewables," said E. R. Brooks, chairman of the utility corporation. "Many people want the option."

Consumers want the option of using more green power, but it has become harder to get. "America gets less electricity from solar, wind and geothermal today than it did five years ago," said Ralph Cavanagh, the energy program director of the Natural Resources Defense Council, an environmental group. Even at its peak in 1987, the industry represented about four-tenths of a percent of the total energy production in this country; today it is about two-tenths of a percent.

CALIFORNIA'S COMMITMENT

A major reason for the decline involves the deregulation of the utilities industry. Many states are opening their utilities to producers and marketers of low-cost electricity, giving customers a choice and perhaps lower rates. California, which passed its deregulation law last fall, will enable corporations, universities and other big customers to choose their energy provider in 1998. It will also guarantee small customers a rate reduction of 10 percent.

Facing competition, many utility companies have become preoccupied with cutting costs, merging with other energy companies, and expanding overseas. Houston's NGC Corporation, a natural gas seller, recently bought Destec Energy, a local power plant operator. Some utilities are restructuring so they can distribute only electricity.

California, which is home, if not a beacon, to many renewable energy companies, provided vital support for green power by prodding utilities to enter into long-range contracts to buy alternative power at high prices. But in 1994 the Federal Energy Regulatory Commission ruled that states cannot force utilities to use renewable energy instead of cheaper sources. Since renewable energy now costs more than that generated by coal, natural gas and nuclear plants, the ruling effectively undermined the industry. Some companies and projects collapsed.

The renewable energy industry is fighting to keep a foothold in the United States; some companies manage by selling wind turbines and solar panels to underdeveloped countries. A flourishing international market has enabled some companies to survive the downturn in this country. Wind and solar power is popular in countries like India and Pakistan where large rural areas are without power plants and extensive transmission systems. Some European countries are also satisfied customers.

There is a bright side to the American quest for alternative energy. With its deregulation law, California is dedicating a little less than 1 percent of every electric bill to supporting research as well as programs for green power; the fund is expected to total about $540 million by 2002. In its fiscal 1997 budget the Clinton Administration has also proposed a sizable increase in funds for research into green sources of power, but the proposal may not survive Congress.

As various states begin pilot programs to investigate electricity deregulation, marketers of power are finding that offering some form of green power is a selling point. While green energy has often turned out to be hydroelectric, which is generated through huge dams that inundate land for miles, its environmental appeal has drawn in utilities and other energy companies. Enron Corporation, a major gas distributor and wholesaler of gas and electricity based in Houston, is trying to turn itself into a national marketer of gas and electricity. It recently added renewable energy to its portfolio by acquiring the Zond Corporation, a California-based developer of wind power.

In the meantime technological improvements in the field are continuing.

The cost of making semiconductor systems has sharply dropped with the use of photovoltaic cells, which convert the energy in light to electricity. Researchers at the National Renewable Energy Laboratory, part of the Department of Energy, have produced a bacterium that cuts the cost of converting waste from agriculture and forestry to ethanol. "Big strides in technology are bringing the cost of power down," Dr. Charles Gay, director of the laboratory, said.

Addressing Environmental Externalities*

Joseph E. Stiglitz,
former Chairman, Council of
Economic Advisers

PRESIDENT CLINTON'S COUNCIL OF ECONOMIC ADVISERS

The notion of tradeoffs is among the most fundamental in economics: nothing is free; everything has an opportunity cost. In private markets, tradeoffs are handled automatically, as consumers choose among alternative goods and services and producers choose among alternative inputs. Prices guide these decisions. Tradeoffs involving the environment cannot be made so easily, however, because use of the environment is generally unpriced. As a result, firms and individuals, in their marketplace decisions, do not always make the best tradeoffs from the standpoint of society as a whole. The effects of failing to price environmental goods and services are examples of externalities (Box 1). When externalities are significant, the government can often design policies that improve the functioning of markets and thereby increase aggregate social welfare.

The Administration has sought to encourage the development of environmental technologies to mitigate tradeoffs and foster economic growth. Improvements in the technologies for preventing and treating pollution, and efforts to spread knowledge about technologies already available, can free resources for other socially beneficial purposes or permit the attainment of higher environmental goals without increasing the burden on the economy. Given the worldwide explosion in environmental regulatory ac-

*This is an excerpt from the *Economic Report of the President* (Washington, DC: Government Printing Office, 1994).

BOX 1   **EXTERNALITIES**

An externality, or spillover, is a type of market failure that arises when the private costs or benefits of production differ from the social costs or benefits. For example, if a factory pollutes, and neither the firm nor its customers pay for the harm that pollution causes, the pollution is an externality. In the presence of this negative (harmful) externality, market forces will generate too much of the activity causing the externality, here the factory's production, and too much of the externality itself, here the pollution. In the case of beneficial externalities, firms will generate too little of the activity causing the externality, and too little of the externality itself, because they are not compensated for the benefits they offer. For example, the development of laser technology has had beneficial effects far beyond whatever gains its developers captured, improving products in industries as diverse as medicine and telecommunications. Too little research and development and other activities generating positive externalities will take place in the absence of some governmental intervention.

To remedy market failures and induce the market to provide the efficient level of the externality-causing activity, the private parties involved in the activity must face the full social costs and benefits of their actions. Policymakers may employ a variety of tools to accomplish this result, such as taxes, user fees, subsidies, or the establishment or clarification of property rights.

---

tivity—in the Far East, in eastern Europe, in Mexico, and elsewhere—the development of more effective and lower cost pollution control technology can also increase our export competitiveness. In fact, we already enjoy considerable success in this area. The United States is now the world leader in exports of environmental equipment. In a global market for environmental technologies of $295 billion in 1992, the $134 billion U.S. share is the largest by far. Our trade surplus in pollution control equipment has been increasing and was $1.1 billion in 1991.

The Administration has also sought to improve the "technology" of regulating the use of natural and environmental resources. This effort involves seeking a better balance among conflicting interests in the use of natural resources, and developing approaches to regulate pollution that rely more on economic incentives and eliminate the economic distortions of some current regulations. Examples of improving the technology for regulating the environment are found in the Administration's plan for managing the old growth forests of the Pacific Northwest, in its approach to grazing on Federal lands, in the Climate Change Action Plan, and in the Administration's position favoring the reauthorization of the Comprehensive Environmental Response, Compensation, and Liability Act, better known as

"Superfund." To better assess where interventions to improve the environment will benefit the economy, the Administration is also engaged in efforts to define sustainable development and develop "green" GDP accounts.

MANAGING RESOURCES ON FEDERAL LANDS

The Federal Government owns vast tracts of land, primarily in the West. These lands contain natural resources of economic importance to both local communities and the Nation, including timber and other forest products, forage for grazing livestock, and mineral deposits. They are also sources of extremely valuable environmental amenities, such as open space for recreational uses like wildlife viewing, scenery, camping, hiking, and hunting; fish and wildlife (including endangered species) habitat; watershed protection; and many others.

Improving the "technology" of regulating the use of these Federal lands is a centerpiece of Administration policy. Two principles guide that policy: (1) reducing inefficiencies caused by improper pricing and regulatory restrictions, and (2) ensuring that both pricing and regulation will achieve a better balance among competing uses of these resources, particularly between extractive (timber, grazing, mining) and environmental uses. These principles can be seen at work in the Administration's plans for managing old growth forests in the Pacific Northwest and for rangeland reform.

Old Growth Forests, Spotted Owls, and Timber

The controversy over logging in the old growth forests and spotted owl habitat of the Northwest provides a case study in reconciling environmental and economic objectives and illustrates how a careful balancing of competing interests can result in progress on all fronts.

The forest products industry is a major industry in the Pacific Northwest, where it is heavily dependent on timber from Federal lands. Much of the Federal land on which this logging has taken place consists of mature forest stands. Referred to as "old growth," this mature forest is the habitat of the northern spotted owl, a threatened species, and many other plants and animals.

For several years Federal forest policy in the Northwest failed to take appropriate account of impacts on environmental quality and biodiversity. In particular, timber harvests on Federal lands were accelerated substantially in the mid- and late 1980s: Such harvests in the habitat of the spotted owl rose from 2.4 billion board feet (bbf) in 1982 to 6.7 bbf in 1988. According to experts, these levels were too high to be sustained indefinitely. Legal challenges to Federal timber policy resulted in injunctions blocking the sale of timber on Federal forest lands in the spotted owl region, in part be-

cause agencies within the Federal Government had failed to work coopera-
tively to comply with environmental and forest management laws. The injunctions had a severe impact on the timber industry, albeit in large part
because harvest levels had been extraordinarily and unsustainably large.

The Administration put a high priority on resolving the problems associated with forest management policy in the Pacific Northwest. Accordingly,
in July 1993, the Administration announced a "Forest Plan for a Sustainable Economy and a Sustainable Environment." The plan attempts to end
the uncertainty caused by legal wrangling and confusion and ameliorate
the impact of economic dislocation, while achieving full compliance with
existing laws. It also seeks to maintain and improve the ecosystem as a
whole, balance the interests of competing uses of the ecosystem for environmental and economic purposes, and create a political consensus to
avoid economic instability.

The plan provides for the maximum legally defensible harvest from Federal forests in the spotted owl region (about 1.2 bbf annually). The process
of adjustment to the new, lower harvest levels will be smoothed by an economic adjustment plan that is expected to create more than 8,000 new jobs
and 5,400 retraining opportunities in the region in 1994. Many of the new
jobs will be in enterprises that improve water quality, expand the prospects
for commercial fishing, and improve forest management in the region.

The plan focuses on maintaining and improving the environmental quality of watersheds in the region, recognizing how the complex interactions
of flora, fauna, and human activities affect that ecosystem. It establishes old
growth reserves and protects over 6.5 million acres of old growth forest
(about 80 percent of existing old growth). It also establishes 10 "adaptive
management areas" for experimentation into better ways of integrating
ecological and economic objectives.

Rangeland Reform

The Federal Government owns extensive rangelands throughout the West.
While these lands are used primarily for grazing cattle and sheep, increased demand for environmental uses has fueled controversy over Federal management. The controversy over rangeland reform shows the
importance of integrating pricing with regulation to use the Nation's resources more efficiently and strike a better balance between economic and
environmental objectives.

A central point of contention involves the fees that the Federal Government charges ranchers to graze animals on Federal land. These fees should
reflect both the value of the forage used by an additional animal and the
external environmental costs of grazing an additional animal (such as
the value of reductions in recreation or water quality). Charging ranchers

the marginal value of forage, the first component, encourages efficient use of the range. By preventing overgrazing, it protects the condition of the range for future grazing uses. It also promotes long-run efficiency in the livestock industry: Prices for forage that are too low encourage excessive investment in the industry. Forage value varies from tract to tract because of differences in forage productivity, location, proximity to roads and other transportation, rainfall, and access to water. But it can still be measured easily and reliably using the value of private rangelands in nearby locations. The second component, the external costs of grazing, cannot be determined from private market transactions. But economists have developed ways of inferring the value of open space or other environmental amenities from the costs people willingly incur to use them or from sophisticated survey methods.

Current Federal management policies are relics of an earlier era when the Federal Government used resource subsidies to encourage settlement of the West. One result is that grazing fees on Federal lands average only 17 to 37 percent of the value of grazing on comparable private lands. Moreover, the formula used to calculate Federal grazing fees has kept those fees from increasing along with private grazing lease rates. Promoting efficiency thus means both increasing grazing fees and ensuring that Federal grazing fees change from year to year in accordance with changes in rent on private grazing land. The Administration's plans for rangeland reform do both. The current proposal calls for phasing in a new fee structure that more than doubles current fees, and for using an updating formula that will adjust Federal fees at the same rate that private fees change.

Pricing reform must be accompanied by changes in regulation. For example, Federal grazing permits have "use-it-or-lose-it" provisions, under which decreases in the number of animals grazed may result in the loss of a grazing permit or a reduction in the number of animals that the permitholder may graze in the future. This policy prevents ranchers from temporarily reducing the number of animals grazed to improve range condition. The Administration's plan allows the terms of grazing permits to be rewritten to allow ranchers to vary the number of animals they graze in response to changes in weather or economic conditions. The plan also includes provisions to strengthen environmental management.

CLIMATE CHANGE ACTION PLAN

Certain gases emitted into the atmosphere by industrial, automotive, and other combustion have been implicated as a threat to the global climate: By preventing reflected solar radiation from escaping into space, these "greenhouse gases" may be causing a generalized warming of the planet. For this reason, an international agreement to reduce greenhouse gas emissions, the Framework Convention on Climate Change, was signed in 1992. The previous Administration had adopted what was called a "no regrets" policy; it was willing to take steps to reduce emissions only if those actions would be beneficial for other reasons—that is, even if greenhouse gas emissions were ultimately found unrelated to changes in the global climate. In contrast, this Administration sees cost-effective policies to reduce greenhouse gas emissions as appropriate "insurance" against the threat of climate change. Accordingly, the President, in his Earth Day speech on April 21, 1993, issued a "clarion call" for the creation of a cost-effective plan to reduce U.S. greenhouse gas emissions to 1990 levels by the year 2000.

The President's call resulted 6 months later in the Climate Change Action Plan, containing nearly 50 initiatives that cover reductions in all significant greenhouse gases and will affect most sectors of the economy. The plan was based on the understanding that the climate change threat results from *all* greenhouse gases, that it depends on *net* emissions (after accounting for greenhouse gas "sinks" such as forests and oceans), and that the problem is *global*. The strategies adopted to address the externalities associated with greenhouse gas emissions were chosen on the basis of a qualitative assessment of the cost-effectiveness of the alternatives, in part by selecting policies that make markets work better.

Some of the strategies expand upon initiatives of this and previous Administrations to promote energy-saving technology. For example, the Green Lights program improves the diffusion of technology by providing consumers and firms with information about environmentally friendly products such as energy-saving lights that promise to reduce electricity generation and the resulting emissions. Other strategies reduce emissions by making government more efficient. Two examples are (1) reform of regulations that block the seasonal use of natural gas (a low-polluting alternative to coal) by electric utilities, and (2) removal of regulatory impediments to private investments in upgrading Federal hydroelectric facilities.

Parking Cashout

Greenhouse gas emissions will also be reduced by improving the pricing of activities that generate externalities. The parking cashout policy attempts to correct a distortion in private incentives resulting from the tax treatment of employer-provided parking. Currently, the Internal Revenue Code allows employers to deduct any costs for employer-provided parking as a business expense, and lets workers exclude the benefits from their taxable income (up to $155 a month). As a result, 95 percent of automobile commuters receive free or subsidized parking, more than half of them in central business districts. All told, U.S. companies claim $52 billion per year in parking-related deductions from this free or subsidized service.

The Climate Change Action Plan proposes that Federal tax laws be modified to require that firms offer employees the option of taking the cash value of their employer-provided parking benefit as taxable income rather than accepting their free parking space. The program would apply initially only to those firms with more than 25 employees that make monthly cash payments for their employees to park in lots owned by third parties. Thus, only about 15 percent of employer-provided parking would be covered at first, although the program would expand later as new parking leases are negotiated.

This policy change should reduce the overuse of automobiles for commuting resulting from the current parking subsidy, by making commuters face more of the social costs of driving. As consumers shift to carpools and public transportation, greenhouse gas emissions, other pollutants, and traffic congestion should all be reduced. Other distortions of the choice between commuting by car and by public transit will remain uncorrected, however, to the extent that current regulation of automobile emissions does not fully capture their environmental, congestion, and health costs.

International Strategies for Greenhouse Gas Reductions

One hundred and sixty-one countries signed the Framework Convention on Climate Change in 1992, agreeing that it is necessary to stabilize greenhouse gas concentrations at a level that will prevent "dangerous anthropogenic interference with the climate system." Because this is a global problem, the Climate Change Action Plan addressed what is termed "joint implementation"—the cooperative effort between countries or entities within them to reduce greenhouse gas emissions. The plan recognizes that there may be enormous cost savings to meeting global goals for greenhouse gas reductions if acceptable international strategies can be developed to reduce emissions where it is cheapest to do so, rather than have each country pursue its emissions reduction goals on its own. Some important questions need resolution, however, such as how reductions are to be identified, monitored, and enforced. To begin testing the joint implementation concept, the plan creates a pilot program that evaluates investments by U.S. firms and government assistance to foreign countries for new greenhouse gas emission reductions; measures, tracks, and scores these reductions; and, in general, lays a foundation for broader, more formal policy initiatives in the future.

SUPERFUND REAUTHORIZATION: THE ADMINISTRATION POSITION

The Comprehensive Environmental Response, Compensation, and Liability Act, better known as Superfund, was enacted in 1980 and amended in 1986 in response to widespread concerns that improperly disposed-of wastes threatened human health and valuable natural resources, such as groundwater aquifers. The act has been unsatisfactory in addressing this problem. Fewer than 20 percent of the 1,300 disposal sites on the priority list drawn up by the Environmental Protection Agency (EPA) have been fully "cleaned up," although 3,500 separate actions have been taken to remove wastes posing an immediate threat to health.

At the same time, the costs of the program have been substantial, running almost $7 billion per year. This figure includes direct draws on the Superfund trust fund collected from the oil and chemical industries to pay for EPA expenses (including $1.6 billion in spending on cleanups where no private parties can be assigned responsibility), $3.2 billion in spending by Federal agencies that own or contributed to hazardous waste sites, and $2 billion in spending by private parties, much of which goes to lawyers' fees and other transactions costs in an effort to escape or reduce liability. Some estimates put the total cost of cleaning up the 3,000 sites projected to be on the EPA's National Priority List (NPL) over the next 30 to 40 years at $130 billion to $150 billion, with $200 billion to $300 billion more needed for Federal facility cleanups.

In response to the poor cost-effectiveness and slow pace of this program, the Administration has proposed several significant reforms. The two most important involve the standards and processes governing the cleanup strategy chosen at a site, and the process for assigning and financing liability.

Remedy Selection

Under the current law, remedial measures at Superfund sites are chosen with a preference for treatment and permanent cleanup of soil and water. They are also selected to meet high standards of cleanliness: land generally must become suitable for residential use, and water often must achieve drinking quality. Costs have little weight in remedy selection; they come into play only to identify the cheapest of the set of remedies meeting other criteria.

The Administration's position establishes more reasonable goals and processes for cleanup decisions. It sets uniform national goals for health and environmental protection to guide remedy selection. It substitutes a concern for long-term reliability as a factor to consider in remedy selection, in place of the preference for treatment and permanence (except for treatment of "hot spots"). It explicitly recognizes containment as a legitimate cleanup strategy. It limits the use of State and Federal standards designed for other pollution contexts. Finally, it introduces greater flexibility and community input into the determination of appropriate land use for the site, permitting some sites to be designated for industrial use, with appropriately lower levels of cleanup required.

The Administration's proposal also offers a streamlined approach to remedy selection at individual sites. With EPA approval, parties will be able to avail themselves of a set of cost-effective "generic" remedies established by the EPA that apply to certain frequently encountered types of waste disposal problems. Alternatively, they can formulate designs that meet national cleanup levels that are based on realistic assumptions and practices concerning risks. If the party liable for cleanup believes it can devise an even cheaper remedy that can meet the national health standards, it can perform a site-specific risk analysis to make its case to EPA. This option allows parties to propose remedies based on the ultimate goal of protecting health and the environment, rather than on the "intermediate" targets of reductions in soil or water concentrations, and helps tailor remedies chosen for a site to its particular features.

Most important, a factor in the remedy selection process at individual sites will be a comparison of the reasonableness of costs against several measures of effectiveness. This approach introduces discipline, transparency, and recognition of tradeoffs into the remedy selection process, while retaining consideration of other factors such as community acceptance and meeting the primary criterion of protecting health and the environment. Cost will also be considered in decisions on whether to defer final cleanups for cases where a new technology is on the horizon to replace a current one that has disproportionately high costs.

The Liability System

The transactions' costs associated with cleanups, especially litigation expenses, have been massive under current law. One study found that these costs account for 19 to 27 percent of all Superfund costs. Transaction costs are substantial in part because liability under current law is strict, joint and several, and retroactive: A party that contributed waste to a site used by others can be held liable for the entire cost of cleanup, and a party is liable for the results of its dumping even if its action was legal at the time. As a result, potentially responsible parties (PRPs) have strong incentives to contest their liability (resulting in high enforcement costs to the EPA), to sue other PRPs to recover costs, and to sue their insurance companies when the latter refuse to pay related claims.

The Administration's proposal seeks to limit these transactions' costs by streamlining the liability allocation process and making it more fair. The new allocation process is based upon nonbinding arbitration, in which PRPs are assigned a share of liability based on factors such as the volume and toxicity of their wastes. PRPs who settle for their assigned shares would surrender their rights to pursue other PRPs for contribution, be protected from suits by other PRPs, and be offered, for a fee, protection from future liability arising from remedy failure or undiscovered harms. As an added incentive to settle, the EPA would pay settling parties for their share of the "orphan shares"—the share of liability attributed to an identified but insolvent party—but nonsettling parties could still be held liable for all or part of the "orphan share."

The Administration proposal also addresses the growing problem of Superfund-related insurance litigation. The problem arises because insurance contracts written before Superfund was enacted did not expressly allocate Superfund liabilities. Subsequently, courts in some States have interpreted those contracts to require insurance companies to assume most Superfund liabilities, but courts in some other States have held the opposite. The scope of insurers' liability in most States is undecided. Building on a proposal originally suggested by the insurance industry, the Administration proposal calls for creation of an Environmental Insurance Resolution Fund financed through fees and assessments on property and casualty insurers. If the PRPs can show sufficient insurance coverage before 1986, the fund would be used to settle their insurance claims for cleanup and restoration costs at pre-1986 NPL sites, as well as some costs at non-NPL sites, at rates determined simultaneously for all of a PRP's sites. The combination of the allocation process and the insurance settlement process should substantially reduce transactions costs and increase fairness.

QUESTIONS FOR ANALYSIS

1. What is the role of externalities in causing environmental pollution?

2. What techniques can the government use to reduce pollution? What are the relative advantages and disadvantages of each of these techniques?

3. Greenpower represented a smaller percentage of total energy production in the United States in 1997 than in 1987. Why?

4. Why did the 1994 ruling by the Federal Energy Regulatory Commission undermine the renewable energy industry?

5. According to President Clinton's Council of Economic Advisers, the fees that the federal government charges ranchers to graze animals on federal land "should reflect both the value of the forage used by an additional animal and the external environmental costs of grazing an additional animal (such as the value of reduction in recreation or water quality)." Why? Aren't federal lands a resource that should be used? Don't ranchers help to pay for federal lands through their tax payments?

6. President Clinton's Council of Economic Advisers criticizes existing government regulations whereby "Federal grazing permits have 'use-it-or-lose-it' provisions, under which decreases in the number of animals grazed may result in the loss of a grazing permit or a reduction in the number of animals that the permitholder may graze in the future." What is wrong with such permits? If the holder of a permit makes little or no use of it, why should he or she continue to have this privilege? Isn't the basic idea to make maximum use of federal lands?

7. President Clinton's Council of Economic Advisers supports a requirement "that firms offer employees the option of taking the cash value of their employer-provided parking benefit as taxable income rather than accepting their free parking space." What is this proposed requirement meant to achieve? Do you think it will work? Why or why not?

8. Is it likely that international cooperation will be required to reduce the emission of greenhouse gases? Why or why not? What problems are likely to be encountered in obtaining such cooperation?

9. From the point of view of society as a whole, shouldn't environmental pollution be eliminated completely? After all, our planet can only tolerate so much in the way of pollutants, and it is common knowledge that air pollution in cities like Los Angeles and water pollution in areas like the Chesapeake Bay are very high. Isn't it obvious that we should put a halt to environmental pollution?

PART SIX

FARM POLICY

Agriculture is an important industry in the United States, and it has been heavily influenced by a variety of government regulations. The first article describes some of the changes in 1996 in federal legislation affecting the country's farms. The second article attacks the approval of a dairy cartel by the Department of Agriculture.

The 1996 Farm Bill*

NEW YORK TIMES

For months, Democrats objected that a Republican-led overhaul of America's farm programs, ending New Deal crop subsidies to farmers and replacing them with gradually declining flat payments over seven years, would shred a valuable Government safety net.

But after a House-Senate panel struck a deal on that very approach this week, President Clinton and senior Congressional Democrats bit their lips and reluctantly agreed to go along.

What happened?

First of all, Congress had to act. The five-year old law had expired, and everyone agreed that reverting to the permanent 1949 law was impractical and far too expensive. Most important, the new Republican majority was convinced that a change to free-market principles in farming was critical to keep the United States competitive in the world market. They also believed that the changes would eventually save money.

The timing was crucial. The nation's 1.5 million farmers were clamoring for a quick resolution because planting season has started in many areas. And no one wanted to alienate farmers in an election year.

But the apparent surrender by the Democrats could also be a tactical retreat. Lobbyists and members of Congress representing those with small farms, which are most vulnerable to market swings, are already regrouping

*This article, by Eric Schmitt, appeared in the *New York Times,* March 24, 1996.

to take another run at the farm bill next year. And if Mr. Clinton is re-elected this fall, he promises, he will lead the charge to protect farmers against natural disasters or price collapses.

"I am firmly committed to working with Congress next year to strengthen the farm safety net," Mr. Clinton said on Friday, "and I plan to propose legislation to do so."

Congress could not have picked a better time to retool the country's agricultural policy. Under the new approach, farmers are guaranteed $4 billion to $5 billion a year in transitional payments through 2002. At the same time, crop prices are at 10-year highs. So farmers win both ways.

"It's easier to look at change in times when you have better prices," said Bill Northey, president of the National Corn Growers Association, representing 30,000 farmers in 25 states, "but I don't think anyone believes that these better prices will be with us for the whole seven years."

That is what many Democrats fear. "When prices decline, and they will, thousands of farmers will be forced off their land," said Senator Kent Conrad, Democrat of North Dakota. "This will not only devastate farms, but also banks and Main Street businesses."

Free-market proponents acknowledge that the new approach carries more risk. But the tradeoff is that most government controls over planting decisions will end, letting farmers grow what they want to take advantage of export markets. Current controls affect only the farmers in the program; many others do not participate and have always been able to plant what they want.

Underlying this approach is the Republican goal of reducing Federal spending. Republicans say their bill will cost more initially than the current program but will save $2 billion over seven years. The bill follows trends in France and many other European countries, which have drastically pared farm subsidies.

"If you look at the big picture over the long term, this will require farmers to use their wits and tools of the marketplace more aggressively," Agriculture Secretary Dan Glickman said in an interview.

Agricultural economists say the new policy will mostly affect small and medium-sized farms, particularly in the Upper Midwest and Southwest, that grow crops covered by the Federal program, like wheat, rice, cotton and corn.

Mr. Glickman said the Administration wanted to develop more innovative "risk-management" mechanisms for farmers and would explore changes with private industry to the often-criticized crop insurance program. The House-Senate panel ended the requirement that farm-program participants buy crop insurance.

The Agriculture Department has started two pilot programs in Iowa and

Nebraska that would safeguard farmers against natural disasters and low market prices. Congressional experts are also looking at various tax-deferred financing mechanisms for farmers.

Democrats are expected to try again to eliminate a cap on the rates of loans that farmers can take out, using their crops as collateral.

The new approach, called Freedom to Farm by its supporters, would accelerate the ongoing consolidation of smaller, less profitable farms into larger, more efficient corporate farms. That has serious implications, not only for the face of farming in America but also for the livelihoods of rural communities.

"The ongoing trend is being driven by changes in technology and in agriculture," said Marvin Duncan, an agricultural economist at North Dakota State University. "Freedom to Farm tends to speed up that process. Whether that's good or bad depends on one's philosophical position."

Dairy Cartel Serves
No Public Interest*

NEW YORK TIMES

Agriculture Secretary Dan Glickman blundered last year when he approved a dairy cartel in the Northeast that would jack up consumer prices by perhaps 25 percent. Fortunately, Mr. Glickman can now make amends. A Federal judge ordered him to show by March 20 that the cartel would, as Congress required, serve a "compelling public interest." Mr. Glickman should admit that he cannot meet that challenge.

The dairy cartel, also called a compact, would control the production and distribution of milk in New England, raising its price by between 13 and 35 cents a gallon. That would pump money into the bank accounts of the region's 3,600 dairy farmers by pushing prices back up to last year's sky-high levels. But it would hit 13 million consumers in Maine, Vermont, New Hampshire, Connecticut and Rhode Island with an added cost of up to $100 million. Poor parents, who spend about twice as much of their income on food as do non-poor families, would suffer the most. Food stamps would buy less milk and other dairy products. High milk prices would also raise the cost of national, state and local nutrition programs.

With Washington cutting money for welfare, food stamps and other poverty programs, this is no time to impose needless costs on the poor. It will be hard for Mr. Glickman to admit he erred when he approved the

*This editorial appeared in the *New York Times* on March 15, 1997.

cartel. But it would be even harder on parents to pay more for their children's milk.

QUESTIONS FOR ANALYSIS

1. In the spring of 1996, prices of corn and wheat were at record levels. Do you think that this was because of rightward shifts of the demand curves for corn and wheat? Why or why not?

2. Do you think that the record prices of corn and wheat were due to leftward shifts of the supply curves for corn and wheat? Why or why not?

3. According to Senator Conrad of North Dakota, "When [farm] prices decline, and they will, thousands of farmers will be forced off their land." Do you agree? If so, is this bad for the country as a whole?

4. The *New York Times* charges that a dairy cartel would increase consumer prices of milk by perhaps 25 percent. Does this seem likely, based on economic theory?

5. If dairy farmers were all poor, and if consumers of milk were all rich, would there still be economic disadvantages in such a dairy cartel? If so, what are they?

PART SEVEN

GDP AND

ECONOMIC

GROWTH

Policymakers have an obvious interest in promoting increases in gross domestic product. To understand what they are up to, you need to know what gross domestic product is. Robert Eisner of Northwestern University describes some of the limitations of existing measures. Edwin Mansfield of the University of Pennsylvania provides evidence that the social rate of return from investments in new technology has been relatively high. President Clinton's Council of Economic Advisers takes up the central question: How fast can the U.S. economy grow on a sustainable basis?

Some Limitations of the GDP Figures*

ROBERT EISNER

The critical definition of final product in the conventional accounts runs into some significant difficulties in its implications for government. Take state expenditures for road maintenance, for example. These outlays, to construction companies and maintenance crews, are by the official definition part of final product—purchases not resold. But is not the final product really the services of the roads, even though these are not generally purchased directly or sold?

Or take police services. Are they final product or are they intermediate product, essential to protecting businesses that produce the final product or to giving consumers a chance to enjoy it? The anomaly may be seen in noting what would happen to our measure of gross domestic product if General Motors were to work out an arrangement with the city of Flint, Michigan, to stop furnishing police protection for its plant in return for an abatement of its property taxes. General Motors would then use what it had paid in these indirect taxes to pay a private protection agency to guard its property. This agency would hire the police released by the city.

Government expenditures for goods and services would then be decreased by the amount of the police salaries. But the cost of producing the automobiles would be unchanged, because payments to the private protec-

*Robert Eisner is professor of economics at Northwestern University. This article comes from his *The Misunderstood Economy* (Cambridge: Harvard Business School, 1995).

tion agency would equal the "indirect business taxes" no longer paid. The value of the output of automobiles would be unchanged. Our measure of gross domestic product would be reduced by the amount of the police salaries, which had been the "final product" of government, even though the only change had been in who paid them—now business instead of government. What had been a final product purchased by government, final because it was paid for in taxes rather than sold, now became intermediate, the sale of services by the private protection agency to General Motors, which in turn resold them as part of its automobiles, which *were* final product.

The final-intermediate product issue turns in the opposite direction in the case of media services financed by advertising. The movie we see in a theater or rent from a video store is valued in final product as what we pay for it. But if we watch the same movie on commercial television, its expense turns up as a cost to the sponsor, a payment, say, by General Motors to ABC television. It is thus "intermediate" in the production and marketing of GM cars, adding nothing to their real value and hence nothing to gross domestic product.

With our conventional official accounts, therefore, gross domestic product goes down as people abandon movie theaters to watch films "for free" on their own TVs. But is their economic well-being really less? Then, if they subsequently abandon free television to subscribe to HBO or Cinemax or rent movies from their local video store, gross domestic product goes up.

Despite the definitions and focus on output for the market, the official accounts actually include a number of "imputations" for the value of output that is not sold in the market. Thus, they add the value of food and fuel produced and consumed on farms. They also include the value of "free" food and lodging provided by employers to employees, particularly domestic workers, and the value of financial services provided to consumers without charge or without charge of full cost, such as free checking services given to depositors in lieu of paying them some or all of the interest earned on their deposits.

Most important, they include the rental values of owner-occupied dwellings. Without this imputation the gross domestic product would go down dramatically as Americans increasingly abandoned the rental market, where the rents they paid were a measure of the housing services in the GDP, to buy new houses or condominiums, where the owners in a sense paid rent to themselves rather than in a market transaction. In effect, the accounts make believe that homeowners are in business. Their business is that of being landlords, who rent to themselves. It is thus that purchases of new houses by these homeowner-businesses are counted as investment, just as is the purchase of a new building by any other business.

Once we admit the need for imputations of some nonmarket production we open up a whole Pandora's Box. There are vast additional amounts of vital services produced by men and, particularly, women in the home, which are not destined for sale in the market. Virtually all of the services of government—whether we like them or not and whether they are paid for by taxes or borrowing—are provided to the public without charge, that is, without market transactions. And we must make many other extensions and revisions of the conventional accounts before we are able to fully measure economic contributions to our well-being, or the effects of debt and deficits on those contributions.

EXTENDED AND REVISED NATIONAL INCOME ACCOUNTS

Consider the old anecdote about the Yuppie who uses some of *his* (note the sexism) high income to hire a housekeeper. He pays *her,* say, $20,000 a year out of his $80,000 salary to keep his luxury apartment in order, to do the marketing and cooking, and generally offer all the comforts he had come to expect from dear old Mom. The Bureau of Economic Analysis, if it included the Yuppie and his housekeeper in its numbers, would find $100,000 of income going into national income. This would correspond to $100,000 of the gross domestic product that they were paid to produce— the $80,000 of advice that the Yuppie gave to clients of his brokerage firm and the $20,000 of housekeeping services produced by the housekeeper.

But suppose that the relationship between the Yuppie and his housekeeper deepens. They fall in love and marry. Our Yuppie now devotes $20,000 a year to meet his wife's personal expenses, which she had previously paid out of her $20,000 salary. What happens to national income and gross domestic product? The BEA will now find the couple earning only $80,000 of national income and contributing only $80,000 to the gross domestic product. While the same services are now being performed—perhaps, with the stimulus of love, more—the national income and product have declined. Activities that entailed "market" transactions are no longer counted because they have become "nonmarket."

HOUSEHOLD WORK AND OTHER NONMARKET ACTIVITY

The story, apocryphal and unrealistic as it may be—it ignores tax considerations, for example—illustrates a vitally important point. Our official conventional accounts omit vast amounts of nonmarket output, particularly within the household. My own conservative estimates suggest that including the value of unpaid labor services in the home would have increased our 1992 gross domestic product of $6 trillion by fully one-third. Think of all the activities we are not counting: child care, cooking, laundering, cleaning, marketing, entertaining—not to mention the value of connubial bliss, which would, if paid for in the market, probably be excluded as illegal, or unobserved, underground activity.

What makes the exclusion of nonmarket activities especially bothersome for serious economic analysis is that they are not a constant proportion of the market activities that are included. Over the past 200 years the economy of the United States has changed from one in which the great bulk of economic activity was nonmarket, e.g., making yarn at the old spinning wheel in the parlor, or growing crops on the frontier farm. Clothes are now store-bought and food comes packaged and even precooked. The bulk of production is sold and bought in the market. The growth in the market economy reflected in the official measures of gross domestic product and national income thus exceeds the growth in the entire U.S. economy, market and nonmarket.

If we compare the United States with less developed countries in Asia or Africa or Latin America, we find that their market economies are much smaller than ours but that the proportion of their output produced outside of the market is much greater. The people of India do not buy many TV dinners. They and the people of other less developed countries are indeed impoverished, but many of them at least are not starving, as they would be if their sustenance were limited to what they could purchase with their few hundred dollars per capita income. Thus, focus on the essentially market activities of the official or conventional accounts tends to exaggerate the long-run growth in developed countries and exaggerates the differences in living standards, though great in any event, between less developed and fully developed economies.

Omission of nonmarket activity from our accounts seriously distorts our measures of a most profound change in the U.S. economy over the past half-century: the massive movement of women into the labor force. Before World War II most women worked in market activities, if at all, until they had children (generally at an early age) and perhaps again after children were grown. Now, most women work for wages and salaries.

The movement of large numbers of women into the labor force has greatly increased market output. But has it increased total output as much? If paid child care is substituted for care by the mother in the home, is that a net increase in child care or output? If restaurant meals are substituted for home cooking, is that an increase in product? If women use part of their market income for commuting expenses, does all of their income properly reflect a net increase in well-being or in output?

Social Rates of Return from R&D*

EDWIN MANSFIELD

By a social rate of return, we mean the interest rate received by society as a whole from an investment. To economists, the social rate of return from investments in new technology is important, since it measures the payoff to society from these investments. A high social rate of return indicates that society's resources are being employed effectively and that more resources should be devoted to such investments if the rate of return stays high. In a series of papers, I have tried to describe the many difficulties in measuring and interpreting the social rate of return. They are numerous and important, but until something better comes along, estimates of this sort are likely to continue to be used.

Although earlier efforts to measure the social rates of return from such investments had been made in agriculture, the first attempt to measure the social rate of return from investments in industrial innovations was published in 1977. The innovations that were included in the study took place in a variety of industries, including primary metals, machine tools, industrial controls, construction, drilling, paper, thread, heating equipment, electronics, chemicals, and household cleaners. They occurred in firms of quite different sizes. Most of them were of average or routine importance,

*Edwin Mansfield is professor of economics at the University of Pennsylvania. This is an excerpt from his paper in *Technology, R&D, and the Economy* (Washington, D.C.: Brookings Institution, 1996).

TABLE 1   Social and Private Rates of Return from Investment in Seventeen Innovations

	RATE OF RETURN (PERCENT)	
INNOVATION	SOCIAL	PRIVATE
Primary metals innovation	17	18
Machine tool innovation	83	35
Component for control system	29	7
Construction material	96	9
Drilling material	54	16
Drafting innovation	92	47
Paper innovation	82	42
Thread innovation	307	27
Door-control innovation	27	37
New electronic device	Negative	Negative
Chemical product innovation	71	9
Chemical process innovation	32	25
Chemical process innovation	13	4
Major chemical process innovation	56	31
Household cleaning device	209	214
Stain remover	116	4
Dishwashing liquid	45	46
Median	56	25

not major breakthroughs. Although the sample could not be viewed as randomly chosen, there was no obvious sign that it was biased toward very profitable innovations (socially or privately) or relatively unprofitable ones. The findings (in Table 1) indicated that the median social rate of return from the investment in these innovations was 56 percent, a very high figure.

To extend this sample and replicate the analysis, the National Science Foundation commissioned two studies, one by Robert R. Nathan Associates and one by Foster Associates. Their results, like those in Table 1, indicate that the median social rate of return tends to be very high. On the basis of its sample of twenty innovations, Nathan Associates found the median social rate of return to be 70 percent. Foster Associates, on the basis of its sample of twenty innovations, found the median social rate of return to be 99 percent.

More recently, Manuel Trajtenberg estimated that the social rate of return to R&D in the field of CT scanners in medical technology was about 270 percent. As he is careful to point out, the interpretation of the gains as social depends on the motives underlying the behavior of hospitals when choosing medical technologies. Also, like hybrid corn, which Zvi Griliches studied, the rate of return would be expected to be high because the innovation was known in advance to be a gusher, not a dry hole. But bearing these things in mind, his results certainly are consistent with the proposition that the social rate of return from investments in new technology tends to be high.

SOCIAL VERSUS PRIVATE RATES OF RETURN

Although the social returns from innovative activities seem to be very high, this does not mean that the private returns—the returns to the innovating firm—are high. In Mansfield et al., whereas the median social rate of return was 56 percent, the median private rate of return was only 25 percent (see Table 1). Also, very rich and detailed data were obtained regarding the return from the innovative activities (in 1960 to 1972) of one of the country's biggest firms. For each year, this firm made a careful inventory of the technological innovations stemming from its R&D and related activities, and it made detailed estimates of the effect of each of these innovations on its profit stream. The average private rate of return from this firm's total investment in innovative activities was about 19 percent, which was much less than the social rate of return.

To understand why the private rate of return from innovative activity is so much lower than the social rate of return, it is important to recognize that the innovator often finds it very hard to appropriate the returns from the innovation. Many of these benefits accrue to imitators, who often obtain information quickly concerning the detailed nature and operation of the new products and processes developed by a firm. According to a study of 100 U.S. firms, this information is in the hands of at least some of their rivals within about a year, on the average, after a new product is developed. For processes, this information leaks out more slowly, but even in the case of processes, it generally leaks out in less than about fifteen months. The major exception is chemical processes, which often can be kept secret for a number of years.

CONCLUSIONS

Practically all the available evidence indicates that the economic payoff to society as a whole from investments in new technology has been very high, the average social rate of return being about 50 percent. There is no assurance that this very high rate of return will be maintained as more and more such investments are made, but thus far there is no convincing evidence that the marginal social rate of return has fallen substantially.

The economic payoff to the innovator is frequently much lower than to society as a whole. Information concerning a new technology leaks out more quickly than is generally recognized. In other than a few areas like pharmaceuticals and agricultural chemicals, the patent system frequently has only a limited effect on the rate of imitation. For investments from which the private rate of return in new technology is low (even though the social rate of return is relatively high), a case may be made for public support.

How Fast Can the U.S. Economy Grow?*

Joseph E. Stiglitz,
former Chairman, Council of
Economic Advisers

PRESIDENT CLINTON'S COUNCIL
OF ECONOMIC ADVISERS

How fast can the economy grow on a sustainable basis? Most mainstream analysts currently believe that aggregate output can grow about 2.5 percent per year. Recently, however, some analysts—perhaps inspired by the outstanding performance of the economy in 1994—have asserted that much more rapid growth, possibly as fast as 5 percent per year, may be sustainable.

The answer to this question has profound implications for the future well-being of the American people. If the mainstream view is correct, aggregate output will double only every 28 years or so, and per capita output only about every 56 years (assuming population growth of 1 percent per year). But if the alternative view is correct, aggregate output could double every 14 years, and per capita output every 18 years.

The answer also has important implications for the conduct of government policy. Sensible Federal budget planning can proceed only in the context of a realistic assessment of the long-term outlook for the economy. If the outlook is robust, then a more expansionary fiscal policy may well be consistent with a responsible outcome on the deficit. If, on the other hand, the outlook is more subdued, a greater degree of fiscal restraint may be required.

*This is an excerpt from the *Economic Report of the President* (Washington, D.C.: Government Printing Office, 1995).

Chart 1 illustrates one simple method for assessing the sustainable rate of growth of gross domestic product (GDP). . . . The chart focuses on the growth of real GDP between the first quarter of 1988 and the fourth quarter of 1994. The reason for focusing on these two quarters is that the unemployment rate was very similar in both: 5.7 percent and 5.6 percent, respectively. This suggests that a similar fraction of the economy's overall productive capacity was being utilized in both quarters. Thus the average rate of growth of output in the interval between them should give a good indication of the average rate of growth of the economy's productive capacity during that period.

As the chart shows, real GDP increased at an average annual rate of 2.1 percent between the first quarter of 1988 and the fourth quarter of 1994. This suggests that the economy's productive capacity—potential GDP— also grew at about that rate. Over the same period, real GDP measured on the more conventional basis (1987 dollars) increased at an average annual rate of 2.3 percent. Therefore, this simple method suggests that the con-

CHART 1 Real Gross Domestic Product

Between the beginning of 1988 and the end of 1994, real GDP increased at an average annual rate of 2.1 percent.

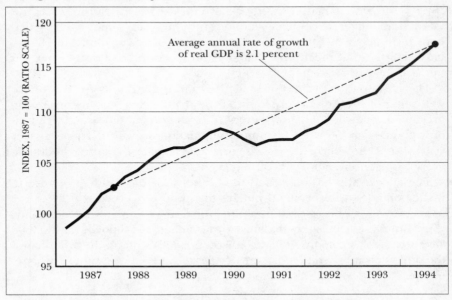

Note: Data are based on a chain-weighted measure.

Source: Department of Commerce.

sensus view that the sustainable rate of growth is about 2½ percent per year is slightly more optimistic than a purely mechanical reading of recent experience would warrant. . . .

FACTORS GENERATING GROWTH OF POTENTIAL GDP

Between 1963 and 1994 real U.S. GDP increased at an average annual rate of 3.1 percent per year. Because the economy appears to have been operating about at its potential in both those years, the average rate of growth of *actual* output between those dates should provide a relatively accurate estimate of the average rate of growth of *potential* output during the same period.

Growth of real GDP can be decomposed into two main components: growth of output per hour worked (or productivity) and growth of hours worked. As Chart 2 illustrates, these two components each contributed 1.7 percentage points to the growth of GDP between 1963 and 1994. (Strictly speaking, the data on productivity and hours worked pertain only to the private nonfarm business sector, whereas the data on output pertain to the

CHART 2 Factors Generating Growth of Gross Domestic Product

Since 1972, real GDP has increased more slowly than before, owing to a reduction in the rate of growth of output per hour worked.

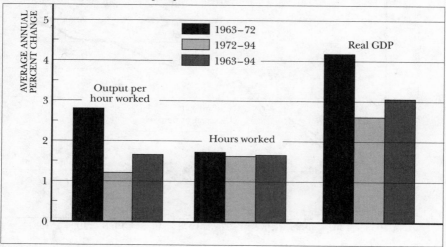

Note: Estimates of growth in output and output per hour are based on chain-weighted measures. Data on output per hour and hours worked pertain to the private nonfarm business sector, whereas the data on GDP pertain to the whole economy.

Sources: Council of Economic Advisers, Department of Commerce, and Department of Labor.

total economy. As a result, and because the output of the private nonfarm business sector was increasing slightly more rapidly than the output of the total economy, the growth of output per hour and the growth of hours worked add up to slightly more than the growth of GDP).

Chart 2 also shows that the average experience since 1963 subsumes two very different episodes. Between 1963 and 1972 real GDP increased at an average annual rate of 4.2 percent. By contrast, since 1972 real GDP has increased only about 2.6 percent per year. (The economy appears to have been operating at about its potential in 1972; as a result, that year should also serve as a useful benchmark for purposes of estimating potential GDP growth rates.) The slower rate of growth of GDP since 1972 can be attributed to a slowdown in the rate of growth of productivity, since the growth of hours worked was about as rapid after 1972 as before.

Chart 3 examines the slowdown in the growth of productivity in more detail. The chart illustrates one of the most significant economic developments of the postwar period. Whereas productivity in the private nonfarm

CHART 3   Output per Hour in the Private Nonfarm Business Sector

Productivity growth in the private nonfarm business sector seems to have slowed markedly sometime in the early 1970s.

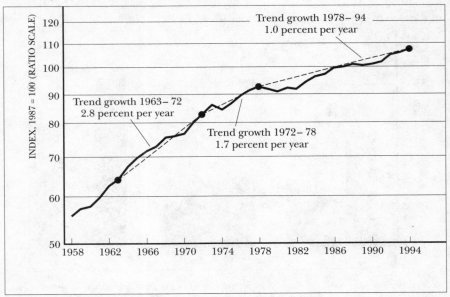

Note: Data are based on a chain-weighted measure.

Sources: Council of Economic Advisers and Department of Labor.

business sector increased at an average annual rate of 2.8 percent between 1963 and 1972, it increased only 1.7 percent per year between 1972 and 1978, and only 1.0 percent after 1978 (yet another year in which the economy was operating close to potential).

By contrast, productivity growth in the manufacturing sector seems to have slowed much less during the past four decades. As Chart 4 shows, output per hour in the manufacturing sector is estimated to have increased on average about 3.3 percent per year between 1963 and 1972, 2.6 percent between 1972 and 1978, and 2.6 percent again between 1978 and 1987. . . .

Taken together, Charts 3 and 4 suggest that the slowdown in the growth of productivity after 1972 was concentrated outside the manufacturing sector. It has been argued that these and similar data exaggerate that concentration, because they do not control for the fact that the manufacturing sector may have increasingly "outsourced" some low-productivity activities. For example, if factories contract with security firms to do work formerly done by their own security guards, that activity will be counted in the services rather than the manufacturing sector, and if security guards'

CHART 4   Output per Hour in the Manufacturing Sector

Productivity growth in the manufacturing sector appears to have slowed only a little since the 1960s and early 1970s.

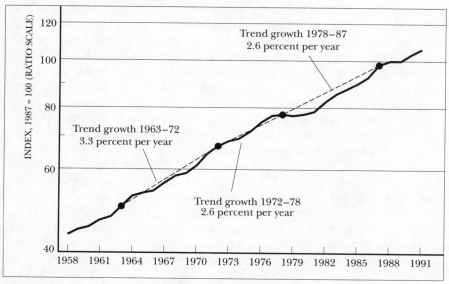

Note: Data are based on a chain-weighted measure.

Source: Department of Labor.

productivity is less than that of the factories' assembly-line workers, official statistics may report an increase in overall manufacturing productivity that does not reflect an increase in the productivity of any individual worker. What this argument ignores, however, is that *high*-productivity jobs may also have been outsourced, in which case the direction of bias in the official estimates would be ambiguous. On balance, the evidence suggests that the apparent strength of productivity growth in manufacturing is not a figment of job migration.

Much of the discussion in this chapter focuses on the slow rate of growth of productivity in the United States since the early 1970s, relative to earlier U.S. experience and the experience of other countries. But it is worth noting that U.S. workers remain among the most productive in the world. This suggests that the productivity "problem" in the United States has much more to do with the rate of growth of productivity than with its level. . . .

HAS THE TREND IN PRODUCTIVITY GROWTH IMPROVED RECENTLY?

Since 1987, according to current estimates, productivity growth in the private nonfarm business sector has averaged 1.2 percent per year, somewhat faster than the average during the previous decade. And since 1991, productivity growth has averaged about 2.0 percent per year—more than twice the 1978–87 average. Are recent claims of a pickup in trend productivity growth justified? (Provided there has been no offsetting reduction in the growth of hours, such a pickup would translate into an increase in the economy's potential growth rate.) This question is not easily resolved because the recent behavior of productivity has been heavily influenced (for the better) by the faster pace of economic activity during the last 2 years. A proper assessment of the trend in productivity growth can be made only by abstracting from cyclical influences.

Chart 5 focuses on the behavior of productivity since 1976. Between 1978 and 1982—a period that included the deepest recession of the postwar period—productivity actually declined slightly according to official estimates. Then, as recovery took hold, productivity rebounded. By 1987 the economy once again was operating in the neighborhood of its full potential. Between 1978 and 1987 the growth of productivity averaged about 0.9 percent per year.

Since 1987 this chain of events has essentially repeated itself: a period of slow growth in productivity as the economy endured a recession, followed by a period of rebound as the recovery gathered strength. Today, well into the expansion, the economy once again appears to be operating in the neighborhood of its potential. Between 1987 and 1994—as was noted above—productivity growth averaged about 1.2 percent per year. Thus,

CHART 5 Output per Hour in the Private Nonfarm Business Sector

Productivity has increased rapidly since 1991. Nonetheless, it is still difficult to know whether there has been an improvement in the trend rate of productivity growth.

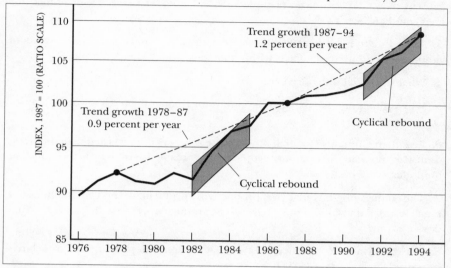

Note: Data are based on a chain-weighted measure.

Sources: Council of Economic Advisers and Department of Labor.

currently available data do seem to hint that the trend in productivity growth has picked up in the last few years. However, the magnitude of that pickup pales in comparison to the decline that occurred earlier in the postwar period. Moreover, the evidence in support of a pickup is still inconclusive. For example, if trends are computed for the periods 1978–86 and 1986–94 rather than 1978–87 and 1987–94, the suggestion of a pickup is much weaker: productivity growth averaged 1.0 percent per year in the earlier alternative subperiod and 1.1 percent in the later one. On the other hand, if the breakpoint chosen is 1988 or, especially, 1989, the evidence in favor of a pickup appears stronger. However, the averages over these later periods, especially the one since 1989, are dominated by the cyclical recovery and so may create a false impression of an improvement in the trend.

Furthermore, the Labor Department released data in 1994 suggesting that the growth of hours worked between 1993 and 1994 may be revised upward by enough to shave 0.1 percentage point off the average rate of productivity increase for the period 1987–94. Thus, while the evidence in favor of a slight improvement in the productivity growth trend is encouraging, it is not yet decisive. The experience of the next few years will be quite telling for this issue.

QUESTIONS FOR ANALYSIS

1. Are police services a final product or an intermediate product?

2. Why does GDP go down as people abandon movie theaters to watch films "for free" on their own TVs?

3. According to Eisner, "our official conventional accounts omit vast amounts of nonmarket output, particularly within the household." Give examples.

4. What is a social rate of return?

5. Why is the economic payoff to an innovator frequently much lower than to society as a whole?

6. President Clinton's Council of Economic Advisers is concerned with the question: How fast can the economy grow on a sustainable basis? Why is this question of fundamental importance?

7. The council suggests that "the productivity 'problem' in the United States has much more to do with the rate of growth of productivity than with its level." What does it mean?

8. Does the available evidence indicate that the trend in productivity growth has improved since the late 1980s?

9. Would you favor public policies designed to increase the rate of productivity growth in the United States? Why or why not?

PART EIGHT

FISCAL POLICY

Everyone who reads a newspaper or watches television must be aware that the United States government spends a huge amount of money. In the first article, John Kasich, who has been the head of the House Budget Committee, describes the changes he favors in government expenditures. Peter Peterson, chairman of the Blackstone Group and former secretary of commerce, argues that entitlements programs like Social Security and Medicare must be cut back, and that the middle class must be prepared for sacrifices.

The People's Budget*

JOHN KASICH

ntitlement programs like Medicare and Medicaid are growing at 10 percent every year; discretionary spending—supposedly limited by "spending caps" enacted in 1990—is growing almost as fast. Literally hundreds of agencies and programs are scattered through the government that simply don't work. And when you add it all up, you have deficits year after year, deficits that have accumulated in a federal debt of nearly $5 trillion.

That debt is one of the reasons change has to occur and has to occur immediately. According to the Joint Economic Committee, a child born in 1995 will pay $187,150 *just in interest payments* on the national debt. Our children will have fewer jobs, pay higher taxes, have lower incomes, and be less able to afford homes because of the debt. By raising interest rates and discouraging investment, the debt is slowing—some would say crippling—our ability to transition into the Information Age economy of the twenty-first century.

The path we are on today is one of slow but certain erosion of America's economic strength. No economy, no matter how prosperous, can afford to pile up literally trillions upon trillions of dollars of debt.

The path we are on today is also fundamentally wrong. It used to be that parents worked hard to pay off the mortgage so they could leave the house to their children. Today, it seems, we are selling off the house and leaving

*This is an excerpt from Edwin Dale, Jeffrey Eisenach, Frank Luntz, Timothy Muris, and William Schneider, *The People's Budget* (Washington, D.C.: Regnery Publishing, 1995).

the children with the mortgage. Balancing the budget is not just an economic issue. It is a moral imperative.

But the budget fight is ultimately about much more than the federal debt. It is about what kind of government we want to have in America. For the last forty years, government has taken power away from the people. The tax burden on the average American family—after adjusting for inflation—has nearly tripled, from $6,970 in 1959 to $18,500 in 1995. Fully half of the average family's income now goes to pay taxes to federal, state, and local governments combined. As the government's budget has grown, the people's budget has shrunk.

Every time government takes a dollar from an American family, it is a dollar less that the family has to spend on feeding, educating, providing health care, and creating a safe and nurturing home for its children. It is a dollar less it has to provide for the parents' retirement or to help out grandparents.

For forty years, the government in Washington has acted as though it, not the American people, was responsible for these things. It has taken money from people to create centralized, bureaucratic programs, run by well-meaning government employees who are asked to do the impossible: design a "one-size-fits-all" government for a country of 260 million people. The simple reality is that it doesn't work and it can't work. It is a matter of common sense: no one can sit in Washington, D.C. and try to tell people in Columbus, Ohio; Austin, Texas; Abilene, Kansas; New York, New York; Detroit, Michigan; and Los Angeles, California the best way to educate children, house the poor, build the roads, and do the literally thousands of other things now dictated from Washington.

The new majority in the House will produce a budget to completely transform the government in Washington. . . . We will:

□ end the myth of federal compassion by sending responsibility for welfare programs back to the states, the localities, and the people;

□ reform the Pentagon to make it more efficient, and revitalize America's defenses and cut foreign aid;

□ cut subsidies to the hundreds of special interests—the privileged, the powerful, and the elite—who have fed for too long at the federal trough;

□ send control over dozens of government activities back to the states, restoring the spirit of the Tenth Amendment of the Constitution;

□ and save the Medicare system from bankruptcy by transforming it into a 21st century system of consumer choice and quality health care.

And when we are done we will have a smaller government, lower taxes, and a balanced budget.

The Third Rail of American Politics*

PETER PETERSON

I can't remember who it was who first said that you could take all the economists in the world, lay them end to end—and still not reach a conclusion. But if you listen carefully to most economists and policy experts today, there is actually a great deal of consensus about the magnitude of America's economic challenges and what sorts of reforms will be necessary to overcome them.

In particular, most would agree to the following: (1) To get American living standards rising again, we must increase productivity. (2) To boost productivity we must invest more—much, much more—not just in machines, but in R&D, in infrastructure, and in people. Many, myself included, think that *at least $400 billion a year in new investments are needed.* (3) This in turn means we must save much, much more—*$400 billion a year more.* (4) The surest and fastest way to increase our savings is to reduce and eventually eliminate the federal deficit, which is really just a form of "negative" public savings. (5) To reduce the deficit and keep it down we must make major cuts in consumption spending, and in particular in entitlements. But this, alas, requires us to confront a brute question: If we are to save more by consuming less, *whose* consumption growth do we propose to cut?

It's at this point that agreement on what needs to be done—while not ex-

*This is an excerpt from Peter Peterson, *Facing Up* (New York: Simon and Schuster, 1994). Peter Peterson is chairman of the Blackstone Group and a former secretary of commerce.

actly breaking down—comes face-to-face with a truth that remains politically inexpressible. That truth is that the problem is all of us. *Most Americans—emphatically including the middle class—will have to give something up, at
least temporarily, to get back our American Dream.*

We all remember Bill Clinton's damning campaign slogan: "It's the
economy, stupid." Well, when it comes to the budget the watchword ought
to be "It's entitlements, stupid." From Social Security and Medicare to farm
aid and federal pensions, it is these benefit programs that dominate the
budget today. In 1993, entitlement outlays totaled a staggering $761 bil-
lion—or 54 percent of all federal spending. And that doesn't include $150
billion more in back-door benefits passed out through the tax code, such as
the deduction for home mortgage interest and the exclusion from taxable
income of employer-paid health care. (These subsidies, which are the fiscal
equivalent of a check in the mail, are technically called "tax expenditures.")

CHART 1   Federal Spending by Major Budget Functions and Federal
Deficit

Entitlement spending dominates the federal budget.

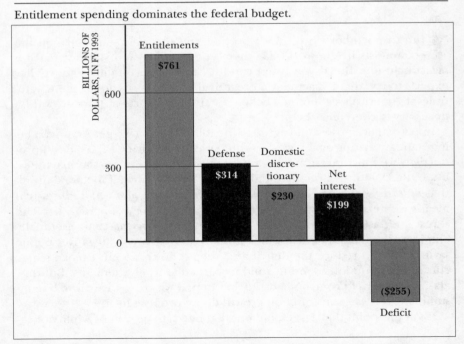

Note: Budget functions are defined by the Congressional Budget Office. Defense includes
"International" discretionary spending.

It is the explosive growth in entitlements, moreover, that threatens to rob our future. I've already noted that even with the Clinton deficit reduction package in place, entitlement outlays are slated to grow by $393 billion in today's dollars between 1994 and 2004. This means that, along with interest costs, they will account for all growth in federal spending over the next decade. In fact, apart from entitlements and net interest, other federal outlays are actually scheduled to decline by $31 billion in real terms between 1994 and 2004. If this seems surprising, recall that the President is aggressively clipping the Pentagon's wings—so that by 1998 we will be spending less on defense, as a share of GDP, than in any year since Pearl Harbor. As for future domestic discretionary spending—for everything from R&D and space exploration to immigration control and law enforcement—this too is expected to shrink as a share of GDP, and by 1997 will have sunk back beneath the postwar record low it reached late in the Reagan administration.

The usual solutions no longer apply. Even if we immediately and permanently cut defense spending by half, twenty years from now we would again

CHART 2   Projected Changes in Federal Spending from FY 1994 to FY 2004 by Major Budget Function

Along with interest payments, entitlements will account for all real federal spending growth over the next decade.

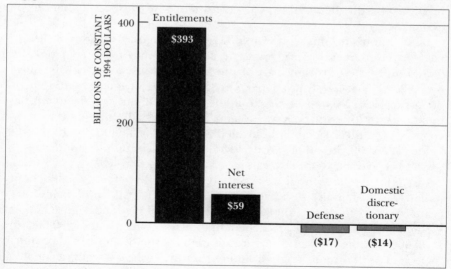

Note: Budget projections by the Congressional Budget Office. Defense includes "International" discretionary spending.

face the same deficit burden as today. We can keep raising tax rates, but to keep up with the growth of entitlements alone we would have to enact a new tax hike, equal to the one sponsored by President Clinton, roughly every four years for the next half century. What we must now confront is the need to cut entitlements.

President Clinton, it's true, never promised to leave all entitlements untouched. But he did make a sweeping social promise that was just as unfortunate in its effects. He assured the public that nothing in his budget would take much away from any household belonging to the "middle class." According to Clinton's definition, moreover, only about 1 percent of all U.S. tax filers—for example, joint-filing couples with gross incomes over $200,000—are too rich to be included in the middle class.

As a guide to tax reform, Clinton's promise was unfortunate enough. Americans with incomes over $200,000 earn just 13 percent of all pretax income in the United States. It shouldn't take any arcane knowledge of fiscal arithmetic to see that balancing the budget on such a narrow stretch of income territory is quite literally impossible. In fact, if President Clinton had wanted to balance the budget by taxing the "rich" alone, he would have had to tax away *all* the taxable income of everyone with more than $175,000 of gross income. Or, taking a less draconian approach, he might merely have *doubled* the income taxes of the "affluent"—but that would have required including everyone down to about $50,000 of income. Even this kinder and gentler approach would amount to something like expropriation—hardly the kind of policy consistent with either free markets or democracy.

But Clinton's promise to the middle class was most damaging in its impact on entitlement reform, since it precluded major savings from the largest and fastest growing part of the budget. Households with incomes over $200,000 received just 1 percent ($5 billion) of federal entitlement outlays in 1991. No one is—or should be—talking about significant entitlement cuts for lower-income Americans. That leaves all households with incomes above the U.S. household median—roughly $30,000 in 1991—yet below $200,000, in other words, that part of Clinton's "middle class," which, however hard-pressed, cannot claim to be destitute.

In 1991, such households received no less than 43 percent of all benefit dollars ($227 billion) disbursed under major Federal entitlement programs. It is worth noting, moreover, that this absolute dollar figure almost certainly understates the total benefit dollars going to the $30,000 to $200,000 income bracket, since it only reflects the 80 percent of entitlement outlays flowing through programs for which we have accurate income data on recipients. What about the remaining 20 percent? We cannot be sure. Some of it flows through programs such as Medicaid, which mostly benefit lower-income households; some too flows through programs such

as student loans, farm aid, and veterans' health care, which disproportionately benefit upper-income households. All told, it would be safe to assume
that total federal benefit outlays reaching the $30,000 to $200,000 income
bracket amounted to at least $265 billion in 1991.

Then consider our ocean of so-called tax expenditures—the subtle subsidies that help Americans borrow huge sums for home mortgages and that
underwrite gold-plated employer health plans. Here the share received by
Clinton's "middle-class" is larger still. Over two-thirds go to tax filers with
incomes between $30,000 and $200,000. Just 7 percent go to the Americans
whom the President calls "rich."

The lesson in these numbers seems clear. Any plan to balance the budget
that exempts the broad middle class from sacrifice is doomed to failure.
But if we are willing to ask for even modest sacrifices from all Americans
with incomes above about $30,000, the picture changes entirely. Suddenly
we're talking about a whopping 73 percent of national household income.
We're also talking about a stunning 74 percent of all tax expenditures and
43 percent of federal entitlement outlays. Taken together, these benefits
amounted to $372 billion in 1991. That's a sum that we simply cannot ig-
nore if we are at all serious about putting our fiscal house in order.

Let's pause for a moment to ask ourselves: What in reality is the "middle
class"? Ask any American if he or she is "middle class," and the answer will
almost always be "yes!" The truly poor will admit to being "lower middle
class" and the rich will go along with "upper middle class," but few will
forthrightly call themselves "poor" or "rich." This is a characteristically
American self-perception, and it reflects our desire to live in a basically
egalitarian society. Next, ask any group of Americans to specify the annual
income that defines "middle class" and you'll hear responses ranging from,
say, $20,000 all the way up to $200,000—if we include the Clinton administration's definition.

But there are more precise and realistic definitions. The median U.S.
household income in 1993 (including nontaxable government and employer benefits) was $31,700. If you narrowly define middle class to com-
prise one-half of all American households, equally distributed around that
$31,700 household, the statistical middle-class income turns out to range
from $14,040 to $55,880.

This exposition regularly startles those who are new to it. A household
with $60,000 of income invariably thinks of itself as "just getting by," but it
actually stands in the top quarter of U.S. households. A two-earner couple
with an income totaling $120,000 may think of itself as just middle class. In
fact, that two-earner couple stands in the top 5 percent of American households. By the time we reach those with incomes in excess of $200,000, we
are left with a mere statistical sliver of the population: roughly 1 percent.

Middle-class Americans today, it seems, suffer from what might be called a "reverse Lake Wobegon" syndrome. As Garrison Keillor fans know, Lake Wobegon is a wonderful fictional place where all the children are *above* average. When it comes to incomes, however, most middle-class Americans, trying hard to make ends meet, assume they must be *below* average.

The broad middle class likes to think that because they aren't genuinely rich, they can't possibly be part of the solution to America's economic problems, and that because they aren't truly poor (aren't a dysfunctional family on welfare, for example), they can't possibly be part of the problem itself. Both lines of reasoning are fallacious. As the accompanying charts show, a huge share of the escalating budget for federal benefit programs is not spent on welfare for the poor, as is commonly thought, but on subsidizing the broad middle class. The truth is that middle-income Americans, just like all other Americans, are on the dole—the entitlement dole. But few realize it. Facing up means facing the fact that we are *all* on welfare of one kind or another.

When middle-class benefits come in the form of Social Security and Medicare payments, or military and civil service pensions, they don't seem like *subsidies* in the sense that welfare checks to the poor are. "I've worked hard all my life; I'm just getting what I am entitled to," middle-class retirees say. And there's exactly the problem! . . . [A] *ll of us* have decided that we are *entitled* to much more than our society can afford to pay for—especially if we want to find the means to invest in our children and our collective future.

QUESTIONS FOR ANALYSIS

1. Do you agree with Mr. Kasich that, "No economy, no matter how prosperous, can afford to pile up literally trillions upon trillions of dollars of debt"? Why or why not?

2. Peter Peterson argues that to increase productivity, we must invest much more, which means we must save more. Why?

3. To save more, Peterson says that we should reduce and eventually eliminate the federal deficit. Why?

4. To reduce the deficit, Peterson contends that entitlements like Social Security and Medicare must be cut. In his view, the problem is that *"[a]ll of us* have decided that we are *entitled* to much more than our society can afford to pay for. . . ."* Do you agree? Why or why not?

5. Is it really necessary that the United States eliminate its budget deficit? Why or why not?

6. Are spending cuts the only way to reduce the deficit? If not, what other ways are there?

PART NINE

TAXATION
AND
PERSONAL
INVESTING

There is considerable interest in tax reform in the United States. The first two articles are a debate between Robert Hall and Alvin Rabushka of Stanford University, who favor a flat tax, and Robert Kuttner of the *American Prospect*, who opposes it. For investors, a related question is: what types of investments are likely to yield high returns? In the final article, Burton Malkiel of Princeton University argues that bonds are likely to be a good investment.

The Flat Tax: Alternative Views

Alvin Rabushka

Robert E. Hall

ROBERT E. HALL AND ALVIN RABUSHKA

Simplify, Simplify*

A surge of interest in complete reform of the Federal tax system is sweeping the country and energizing Washington. One source of the desire for change is disgust with the hideously complex tax system we now have. Another is the higher economic growth that a consumption tax would bring. And a third is the anger that honest taxpayers feel about widespread tax avoidance and tax evasion in the current system.

But the public also wants to retain one important feature of the existing system: progressivity, the principle that people with higher incomes should pay a higher percentage of that income in taxes. In particular, the poor should be exempt from tax up to a reasonable level of sustenance. The nation is ready for a simple, easily enforced, progressive tax on consumption.

For more than a decade, we have been advocating a tax reform with all of these features. Both the structure of the tax and estimates of its revenue have withstood close examination by experts, including the Treasury. The tax would reproduce the revenue of the current personal and corporate taxes with just a 19 percent rate. Our idea has generally been called the flat tax. But there is much more to it than just a simpler tax schedule.

One of the most important principles is to tax business income where it is generated—in businesses—rather than after it makes its way to individual

*This article appeared in the *New York Times* on February 8, 1995. Robert Hall and Alvin Rabushka are senior fellows at the Hoover Institution at Stanford.

119

taxpayers in the form of interest and dividends. Right now the system allows businesses to deduct such items, then tries to collect taxes from the recipients—an inefficient procedure that invites fraud.

To tax income at its source, we propose a comprehensive business tax. It would replace the current corporate income tax, personal taxes on noncorporate businesses and personal taxation of interest and dividends. Think of it as a withholding tax on interest, dividends and other types of income people earn from business. At the individual level, we'd tax only wages, salaries and pensions.

Here is where the system is progressive—a family of four pays tax only on earnings above an exemption level of $25,500. A family earning $25,000 pays no individual tax; one earning $50,000 pays $4,655, and one earning $100,000 pays $14,155. Dividends and interest have already been taxed at the business level and are not taxed again.

And the gains in simplicity are immense. Businesses and families can file their returns on forms the size of postcards. The numbers entered on these forms are clear and easy to calculate. Opportunities for evasion are minimized. The resources needed to comply with this streamlined tax system are a tiny fraction of those consumed today by Federal income taxes.

A family would pay a 19 percent tax on the amount that its wages, salaries and pensions exceed the exemption level. A business would pay a 19 percent tax on its revenue, with deductions for purchases of materials from other businesses; for its wages, salaries and pensions, and for its purchases of capital goods.

These deductions are central to the design of the tax. The deduction for materials bought from other businesses guarantees that business income is taxed once and only once. The deduction for wages, salaries and pensions recognizes that families pay taxes on these earnings. And the deduction for purchases of capital goods (plant and equipment) makes the tax a consumption tax.

Why do the family and business taxes add up to a consumption tax? Consumption is total income minus investment in new capital. Any tax imposed on income minus investment is a consumption tax.

There are many economically equivalent ways to administer a consumption tax. One obvious way would be a national sales tax on consumption of goods and services. The trick would be to make the sales tax progressive; that would require something like a family rebate of the tax on purchases up to an exemption level. But rebates create enormous opportunities for fraud. Even today, the Internal Revenue Service is battling a huge stream of fraudulent applications for tax refunds. The taxes we propose would be the equivalent of a 19 percent Federal sales tax together with a fraud-free rebate based on earnings.

Another way to set up a consumption tax is a value-added tax—the equivalent of a sales tax, collected along the way from businesses at every stage of production instead of the point where goods are sold to consumers. The entire tax is collected from businesses; individuals don't file tax returns. Value-added taxes are universal in Europe and have proved that broad taxes on consumption are feasible. But like a sales tax, a VAT is not progressive: it taxes a family's consumption from the first dollar. The only way to make it progressive is to issue rebates, and this opens the door for fraud.

The last way to set up a tax on consumption is to impose a tax on individuals, measuring consumption as what they earn minus what they save. Like our plan, the individual consumption tax is progressive without a rebate because it has a tax form for individuals and taxes are limited to the amount of consumption over an exemption level.

But an individual consumption tax would be an administrative nightmare. Not only would individuals have to report all types of income (rather than relying on universal withholding), but the IRS would have to keep track of billions of new items to measure saving. Dishonest taxpayers would overstate their payments into savings accounts and understate their withdrawals. True simplification and efficiency cannot be achieved with a family consumption tax.

Consider the goals we started with. Tax only consumption. Tax it progressively. Make it easy to comply and hard to commit fraud. The system embodied in our two post-card-sized forms is the unique proposal that delivers them all.

The Flat Tax: Alternative Views

ROBERT KUTTNER

Instead, Close Loopholes*

Tax all business and personal income at a flat rate, say 17 or 19 percent. Eliminate all deductions, depreciation schedules and other complications. Raise the personal exemption, so moderate-income households pay little or no tax. It sounds wonderful.

But on closer examination, the logic of such "flat tax" plans falls apart. Behind the promise of simplicity and tax reduction are higher deficits and a more regressive tax system.

The leading proposal on the table right now is by Representative Richard Armey of Texas, the House majority leader. As drafted, it would cost the Treasury more than $200 billion a year. To be truly revenue-neutral, it would require a rate of more than 25 percent, increasing taxes on all but the wealthiest payers.

The silliest part of the "flat tax" notion is the very premise that simplification requires a single rate. Tax rates, of course, are not what makes taxation complex. For individuals and businesses, calculating the rate is the easy part. Whether the schedule is flat or graduated, you just multiply taxable income by the applicable rate. The complicated part is figuring out what constitutes taxable income—what should be deducted, if anything, before you calculate your taxes.

*This article also appeared in the *New York Times* on February 8, 1995. Robert Kuttner is co-editor of the *American Prospect*.

Eliminating deductions would obviously simplify the tax system. But some tax preferences, like the mortgage interest deduction, serve good social purposes, and others, like the deduction for medical expenses, reflect the fact that if you earn $60,000 and have to spend $30,000 on doctor and hospital bills, you don't have the same resources as a healthy person who makes $60,000. Mr. Armey would do away with both.

Businesses' taxable income, likewise, is no simple matter to calculate. If we swept away the complex treatment of business income and expenses, a lot of businesses would be taxed on their expenses as well as their profits.

The more serious mischief in the flat tax campaign is the tired claim that we can have a free lunch: lower taxes for most people and no effect on the budget. Mr. Armey says this is possible since "as the economy grows because of the favorable treatment of savings, investment and low marginal tax rates, revenue to the Treasury will grow."

If this sounds familiar, it's because under its old name—supply-side economics—it was discredited by a full field test in the 1980s. Ronald Reagan's supply-side tax cuts never delivered their promised revenue increases; deficits became chronic and the national debt tripled. Conversely, during the long postwar boom, rates on the richest taxpayers were as high as 91 percent and the economy did just fine. And ever since the top tax rate was raised in the 1993 budget accord, the economy has been growing at least 4 percent a year.

The Treasury Department calculated last fall that far from raising more money, a flat tax of 17 percent would reduce tax receipts by $244 billion a year. Mr. Armey complained that the Treasury had misunderstood certain technical aspects of the bill, such as the interaction of income and payroll taxes. Treasury disagreed, but found that even accepting Mr. Armey's technical adjustments, the plan would still lose $186 billion a year.

An analysis by Citizens for Tax Justice, based on the Treasury findings, calculates that a revenue-neutral version of the Armey plan would require a flat rate of 25.8 percent. That would mean higher taxes for every income group—except people making $200,000 or more. That group would enjoy an average tax cut of $28,410.

Mr. Armey's plan, like other such proposals, was inspired by the economists Robert Hall and Alvin Rabushka, whose 1983 book *Low Tax, Simple Tax* promised similar miracles (with similar mathematical ingenuity). But even Mr. Hall has been quoted as estimating that the Armey plan would require a 23 percent tax rate to break even; and the Hall-Rabushka book acknowledged that a flat tax would be "a tremendous boon to the economic elite" and that "lower taxes on the successful will have to be made up by higher taxes on average people."

The tax system can be greatly simplified without giving up graduated rates. The 1986 Tax Reform Act, sponsored by Representative Richard Gephardt of Missouri and Senator Bill Bradley of New Jersey, cut rates top and bottom, and paid for the cuts by closing loopholes. President Clinton's 1993 tax amendments paid for tax relief at the bottom by raising rates at the top.

There are still plenty of loopholes that don't make economic sense. Large inheritances are so shielded from taxes that the estate tax is mostly, as a Brookings Institution study dryly termed it, "voluntary." Tax breaks for second homes and lavish deductions of business expenses can be eliminated to cut taxes on working families.

Nobody likes taxes. But if we are to have public services at all, it makes sense to pay for them by taxing wealthy people at higher rates than the middle and working class. Mr. Gephardt, now the House minority leader, recently proposed that by closing additional loopholes, we could reduce rates and yet retain a system at least as progressive as the current one. The Gephardt approach has been described in some quarters as a Democratic flat tax, yet another case of Democrats embracing Republican ideas. It is not. It is a marriage of tax simplification and tax fairness—without raiding the Treasury.

The very idea of a flat tax is a reversal of the well-established principle of taxation based on ability to pay. Progressive taxation dates to Woodrow Wilson. It is sensible economics, popular politics and sound fiscal policy. Democrats would make a big mistake to borrow the "flat tax" concept—or the label.

Bonds Are Good Investments*

BURTON MALKIEL

L et's now turn to an assessment of the bond market. High-quality corporate bond yields, while well below the early 1980s peak, were in mid-1995 around 8 percent and still reasonably generous. Remember that inflation rates have also come down sharply. While it is true that the measured rate of inflation in the United States rose to about 5 percent at the end of the 1980s, recent wage behavior and productivity trends suggest a core inflation rate at the start of 1995 of no more than 3 to 4 percent. This gives a projected very generous real rate of return of something in the vicinity of 4 to 5 percent, not too much lower in real terms than earlier in the eighties. Thus, bonds in mid-1995 were priced to be a very serviceable investment that should provide unusually generous real rates of return. Over the long pull in the United States, corporate bonds have historically produced a real rate of return of only 2 percent, as measured by Ibbotson and Sinquefield.

Comparisons of prospective stock and bond yields can potentially be very helpful to investors. The following figure plots bond yields and prospective rates of return on common stocks (the Dow Jones industrial average), calculated using the growth-rate estimates of Wall Street analysts. The figure shows that bond yields rose above the prospective returns from stocks only

*Burton Malkiel is professor of economics at Princeton University. This is an excerpt from his *A Random Walk Down Wall Street*, 6th ed. (New York: Norton, 1996).

CHART 1   Expected Total Return: Stocks and Bonds

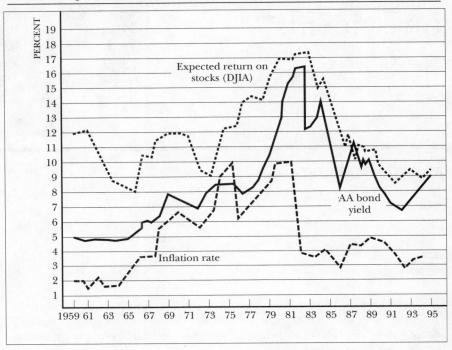

once. That was during the early autumn of 1987. When even U.S. government bonds rose above 10 percent, this proved far too competitive for common stocks and the market collapsed. While I would never claim that any statistic can reliably predict turns in the market, such comparisons can at least be helpful in providing warning signals and revealing periods of attractive relative values in the bond market. As of mid-1995, bonds appeared to offer return possibilities almost as attractive as stocks but with less risk.

Bonds are the Rodney Dangerfield of financial investments. They don't get much respect. The arguments against bonds are easy to make. Over the long pull, their total return (interest payments plus capital gains and losses) has been far inferior to that of common stocks. Over the past sixty years, stocks have returned a compound annual rate of 10 percent, about 7 percentage points better than the average rate of inflation over the period. On the other hand, high-grade corporate bonds have eked out a rate of return of only about 5 percent. In inflation-adjusted terms, bonds yielded 2 percent versus 7 percent for stocks; thus, stocks did 3½ times as well as bonds.

With the benefit of hindsight, we now know that bonds were inappropriately priced thirty years ago (as they also were in the forties and early fifties when their yields were pegged at artificially low levels). If investors had known thirty years ago that inflation would become a major problem—if they had correctly forecast that the general economy, inflation rates, exchange rates, and, therefore, interest rates would become increasingly volatile—bonds would not have been priced to give such inadequate total returns. But remember that our smartest economists were claiming in the early 1960s that inflation (then at 1 percent) was dead and that even minor fluctuations in economic activity could easily be offset. Economists and investors were egregiously wrong. But they are not likely to be wrong forever.

The point is that you shouldn't invest with a rearview mirror. What was a poor investment over the past sixty years will not necessarily be one over the next sixty. Investors learn, and new information about inflation and volatility does get incorporated into market prices. Bonds today reflect the poorer inflation outlook and the greater instability of bond prices. The issue is not how poorly bond investors fared in the 1950s, 1960s, and 1970s. The issue is: Will bonds produce a generous return in the future? I believe that when purchased at the 8 percent yield levels existing as of mid-1995, the answer is yes. . . .

COULD I BE WRONG?

The thesis presented is that at the price levels existing in mid-1995, attractive prospective returns are likely to come in the future from investment in bonds. Stocks appear to be, at best, of average attractiveness. A popular maxim warns, however, "If you can remain calm when everyone around you is panicked, perhaps you don't understand the problem." Could the problem be worse than I have described? Could the market actually be underestimating the long-run inflation dangers to economic instability? What if the core rate of inflation is about to ratchet back up to the double-digit level, as some investors fear? This is precisely the situation that would make my investment thesis wrong as it concerns long-term bonds. (And it would undoubtedly make investment in tangible assets far more attractive than was the case in the 1980s.) So the critical final question I must address is the likelihood that the current core inflation rate will remain at a restrained level.

While many forecasters anticipate a sharp acceleration of inflation in the late 1990s, I would suggest to you that there are at least some reasons for optimism as well as some for concern. The most favorable part of the picture concerns the behavior of wage settlements. Average hourly earnings are still rising at less than a 4 percent rate. I realize that many analysts believe that the recent period of wage restraint is an aberration and that a significant acceleration of wage settlements is likely. But even if this were true, the tightening of controls throughout American industry and the increasing experience mix of our labor force augur well for a better productivity performance in the late 1990s. Thus, the rise in unit labor costs (which I have suggested is a good proxy for the core rate of inflation) should not increase by more than 4 percent and may do even better.

Over the longer term, however, there are also reasons to be sanguine. I think we have learned throughout the Western world that our economies do not work well with high and variable rates of inflation, and there is now a willingness to accept far harsher demand management policies than was previously thought politically feasible. The level of unemployment throughout the Western world was higher in the mid-1990s, and was expected to stay higher than at similar points of postwar economic cycles. Moreover, even socialist European Economic Community countries were experiencing unprecedented high rates of unemployment. While there should be considerable growth in the less-developed world and in formerly communist countries, it seems quite likely that the world economy will not be characterized by excess demand and increases in the prices of basic commodities. Our past problem with inflation was associated with worldwide excess demand or at least tight supply conditions.

Moreover, U.S. labor clearly recognizes that our economy is now sufficiently open to world trade that continued reasonable moderation in industrial wage demands and acceptance of changes in work rules are essential if we are to keep from becoming a service economy. An industry-by-industry analysis suggests that heightened competitive pressures in both domestic and foreign markets (and including substantially increased competition from developing countries) have significantly changed the wage-setting process. Moreover, the deregulation of such industries as airlines, trucking, and telephone service has triggered increased wage competition in many industries. While no one can tell if we will succeed, there are certainly reasons for optimism that the upward ratcheting of the core inflation rate has ended.

There is, however, one disturbing part of the picture that has not yet fallen into place in the United States and is, I believe, the reason interest rates are still as high as they are and threaten to return to even higher levels. The projected federal budget deficit in the mid-1990s is still far too large. More disturbing is the fact that most projections show the deficit rising in the late 1990s with the aging of the U.S. population. It is clear that political action with respect to the budget will be necessary to remove the legitimate fear that interest rates will increase as private and federal demands overwhelm the supply of savings or that continued deficit spending will eventually lead to inflation. Progress on the deficit would remove an important question mark on the thesis presented, at least as it concerns investment in bonds. Even if less progress is made than desirable, I believe that bonds will provide reasonable real rates of return over the remainder of the 1990s. At the very least, investors should assign some substantial probability to this continued moderate inflation scenario (or at least no return to the 1970s inflation scenario) and balance their equity positions with some portion of their investment funds in bonds.

It is also well to remember . . . that capital markets are at least reasonably efficient over the long pull. Fears about renewed inflation and economic instability are not reflected in stock and bond prices at some time in the future; they are reflected in the market now. If investors perceive that investment risk has increased, the financial pages reflect such thinking very quickly. In well-functioning financial markets, such as ours, investors are willing to buy only those assets that will provide the higher future rates of return sufficient to compensate them for added risk.

Does my expectation for reasonably attractive rates of return from bonds and stocks mean that I am predicting a bull market rally during some specific period of the late 1990s? Not at all! As a random walker through Wall Street, I am skeptical that anyone can predict the course of short-term stock price movements, and perhaps we are better off for it. I am reminded of one of my favorite episodes from the marvelous old radio serial "I Love a Mystery." This mystery was about a greedy stock-market investor who wished that just once he would be allowed to see the paper, with its stock price changes, twenty-four hours in advance. By some occult twist his wish was granted, and early in the evening he received the late edition of the next day's paper. He worked feverishly through the night planning early-morning purchases and late-afternoon sales which would guarantee him a killing in the market. Then, before his elation had diminished, he read through the remainder of the paper—and came upon his own obituary. His servant found him dead the next morning.

Since I, fortunately, do not have access to future newspapers, I cannot tell how stock and bond prices will behave in any particular period ahead. Nevertheless, I am convinced that the long-run estimates of bond and stock returns presented here are the most reasonable ones that can be made for investment planning during the remainder of the 1990s and into the twenty-first century. Investors will, I believe, be well served by putting their money where my mouth is and investing a substantial part of their wealth in paper assets, including bonds.

QUESTIONS FOR ANALYSIS

1. Professors Hall and Rabushka argue for a tax on consumption expenditure, not on income. What are the advantages of such a tax?

2. Mr. Kuttner argues strongly for progressive taxation—that is, for the principle that tax rates should be higher for the affluent than for the poor. Do Professors Hall and Rabushka reject this argument?

3. According to Professors Hall and Rabushka, their form of a flat tax is preferable to a value-added tax. Why?

4. Why are bonds the "Rodney Dangerfield" of investment?

5. Explain why Professor Malkiel believes that bonds are a good investment.

PART TEN

MONETARY

POLICY

In the late-1990s, there was considerable and continuous controversy over monetary policy. Many observers believed that the Federal Reserve's policies were not sufficiently expansionary; others felt that the opposite was true. The first article in this part is the testimony of Alan Greenspan, chairman of the Fed, before the Senate Banking Committee in 1997. The second article is a wide-ranging discussion of central bank independence and other topics by James Tobin of Yale University. The third article, by Alan Blinder, discusses what the Federal Reserve's objectives should be.

The Fed Must Be Sensitive to Imbalances*

ALAN GREENSPAN

The members of the F.O.M.C. (Federal Open Market Committee) expect inflation to remain low and the economy to grow appreciably further. However, as I shall be discussing, the unusually good inflation performance of recent years seems to owe in large part to some temporary factors, of uncertain longevity. Thus, the F.O.M.C. continues to see the distribution of inflation risks skewed to the upside and must remain especially alert to the possible emergence of imbalances in financial and product markets that ultimately could endanger the maintenance of the low-inflation environment. Sustainable economic expansion for 1997 and beyond depends on it. . . .

The willingness of workers in recent years to trade off smaller increases in wages for greater job security seems to be reasonably well documented. The unanswered question is why this insecurity persisted even as the labor market, by all objective measures, tightened considerably. . . .

Certainly, other factors have contributed to the softness in compensation growth in the past few years. The sharp deceleration in health care costs, of course, is cited frequently. Another is the heightened pressure on firms and their workers in industries that compete internationally. Domestic deregulation has had similar effects on the intensity of competitive forces

*This testimony was presented before the Senate Banking Committee on February 26, 1997. Alan Greenspan is chairman of the Board of Governors of the Federal Reserve System.

in some industries. In any event, although I do not doubt that all these factors are relevant, I would be surprised if they were nearly as important as job insecurity. . . .

The F.O.M.C. has recognized the need to remain vigilant for signs of potentially inflationary imbalances that might, if not corrected promptly, undermine our economic expansion. The F.O.M.C., in fact, has signaled a state of heightened alert for possible policy tightening since last July in its policy directives. But we have also taken care not to act prematurely. The F.O.M.C. refrained from changing policy last summer, despite expectations of a near-term policy firming by many financial market participants. In light of the developments I've just discussed affecting wages and prices, we thought inflation might well remain damped, and in any case was unlikely to pick up very rapidly, in part because the economic expansion appeared likely to slow to a more sustainable pace. In the event, inflation has remained quiescent since then.

Given the lags with which monetary policy affects the economy, however, we cannot rule out a situation in which a pre-emptive policy tightening may become appropriate before any sign of actual higher inflation becomes evident. If the F.O.M.C. were to implement such an action, it would be judging that the risks to the economic expansion of waiting longer had increased unduly and had begun to outweigh the advantages of waiting for uncertainties to be reduced by the accumulation of more information about economic trends. . . .

Clearly, when people are exposed to long periods of relative economic tranquillity, they seem inevitably prone to complacency about the future. This is understandable. We have had 15 years of economic expansion interrupted by only one recession—and that was six years ago. As the memory of such past events fades, it naturally seems ever less sensible to keep up one's guard against an adverse event in the future. Thus, it should come as no surprise that, after such a long period of balanced expansion, risk premiums for advancing funds to businesses in virtually all financial markets have declined to near-record lows.

Is it possible that there is something fundamentally new about this current period that would warrant such complacency? Yes, it is possible. Markets may have become more efficient, competition is more global, and information technology has doubtless enhanced the stability of business operations. But, regrettably, history is strewn with visions of such "new eras" that, in the end, have proven to be a mirage. In short, history counsels caution. . . .

Why should the central bank be concerned about the possibility that financial markets may be overestimating returns or mispricing risk? It is not that we have a firm view that equity prices are necessarily excessive right now or risk spreads patently too low. Our goal is to contribute as best we can to the highest possible growth of income and wealth over time, and we would be pleased if the favorable economic environment projected in markets actually comes to pass. Rather, the F.O.M.C. has to be sensitive to indications of even slowly building imbalances, whatever their source, that, by fostering the emergence of inflation pressures, would ultimately threaten healthy economic expansion.

Central Bank Independence and Other Topics*

JAMES TOBIN

QUESTION: Recently, there have been calls for more congressional control over monetary policy and central bank operations. What is your view on the question of central bank independence?

TOBIN: I think some aspects of the Federal Reserve are inconsistent with democratic political theory, and I will tell you what they are. These are views that I've published and voiced in hearings in Congress. I don't think that there should be votes on the Federal Open Market Committee for people who are not appointed as public servants by the president and who are not subject to confirmation by the Senate. I think either the bank presidents should have no votes, or, to achieve voting status, they should be appointed and confirmed in the same manner as the governors. That doesn't make me popular with the presidents of Reserve banks, but that's what I think. Personally, I have nothing against the presidents of Reserve banks, I think most of them would be perfectly good people to have the president appoint and the Senate confirm. I just think it's contrary to democratic politics to have private citizens voting on the most important questions of macroeconomic policy.

I also think that the four-year term of the chairman of the Fed and the

*This is an excerpt from *The Region* (Minneapolis: Federal Reserve Bank of Minneapolis, December 1996). James Tobin is professor emeritus of economics at Yale University.

four-year term of the president should be better synchronized. I think the fact that it's not is completely accidental, it just got that way because of bad drafting of the law. Now, though, we have this anomaly that when a new chairman is appointed he's appointed for four years from that date. He's not appointed to fill out a term which has fixed dates of starting, as are the governors. Maybe six months after the president's term begins the chairman's term should begin, or maybe a year, but not three-and-a-half years the way it is now. I wrote an op-ed piece in the *Wall Street Journal* last March when Greenspan was being reappointed, where I suggested we make this kind of change by appointing Greenspan only for what would be logical for starting a new four-year term, and get on to a better rhythm.

I also suggested that we go back to the practice, as before 1933, of having the Secretary of the Treasury on the Board, and I would add the Chairman of the Council of Economic Advisers.

QUESTION: You would put the Treasury Secretary back on?

TOBIN: Put him back on and the Chairman of the Council, too. Put them on, at least, for being present, even if they don't have votes. I'm not trying to do anything drastic, I just think the present system is too antidemocratic.

QUESTION: Some might argue that such moves would too closely link the Fed and the White House, that it would politicize monetary policy.

TOBIN: Well, you see, it's not just a technical question. It's not as if monetary policy is nonpolitical. Monetary policy is politics. The judgments, the trade-offs involved during the 1979–1980 policies, for example, or during any deep recession, are not just technical matters. The president is blamed and credited for what happens to the economy, but what happens is not done by him. Clinton is the beneficiary of Greenspan's success, but he might have been the victim of Greenspan's failures in policy. But either way he, perhaps, should have a little more to say about what goes on—as the president used to have. It used to be that the chairman of the Fed resigned when a new president came in. No longer.

QUESTION: The *1962 Economic Report of the President,* which you helped write, was considered by some to be a Keynesian manifesto; 34 years have passed since that report was written and other economic ideas have since then made their mark, such as monetarism, rational expectations and supply-side economics. What is the current state of Keynesian economics?

TOBIN: The Keynesian economics that I was talking about, circa 1962, was not just what was written in the *General Theory* in 1936, but was a result of an evolution of the subject between those two dates. For example, there's one whole chapter of that document on growth, long-run growth, not on Keynesian macro. And I think it looks pretty good still, but I'm prejudiced.

I think Keynesian ideas are still what's going on in practical economics. What guides the Federal Reserve mostly is mainstream Keynesian macroeconomics. I don't see monetarism being of any practical use these days and I don't see real business cycle theory being of any practical use any days, even though it occupies an inordinate amount of time of some very gifted people and their students. And supply-side economics, aside from the supply-side economics that is just ordinary microeconomics and growth economics, the supply-side economics that you might call "pop" supply-side economics which, unfortunately, was able to get a certain amount of authenticity in this most recent political campaign for an outrageous proposal by Sen. Dole, I don't see any of that getting anywhere at all. So, Reaganomics, supply-side economics in that sense, Laffer curves, Jack Kemp stuff, alas the stuff that some very good economists were selling during the recent campaign, that's nonsense and that's certainly not getting us anywhere. So after you look at the other entries in the beauty contest, you come back to the natural evolution from 1936 to 1962. . . .

QUESTION: Research produced at the Federal Reserve Bank of Minneapolis was instrumental during the early years of rational expectations theory. What is your assessment of rational expectations, and has it aided in the formulation of policy?

TOBIN: I think I just answered that—I don't think it has helped in the formulation of policy. I do think there is a good idea involved, an idea that's unexceptional in that it's a canon for model building, that is, you should have expectation-consistent models, or model-consistent expectations—in the sense that you should not build a model that says people are behaving incorrigibly with expectations that are not justified by the model itself. I think that canon is met by almost all long-run models—that was always the characteristic of those models. Now, where problems come is finding the model-consistent expectations in a business cycle, where things are changing a lot. And there I think that the ambitious program of saying, "Let's see if we can generate moving equilibrium systems in which we have model-consistent expectations and uncertainty," and so on, that has proved to be an over-ambitious program that hasn't paid off yet. Maybe it will; meanwhile, I see Lucas and Prescott not working on that anymore.

QUESTION: You have been critical of minimum wage laws, arguing that the intended beneficiaries are not likely employed because they lack the capacity to earn a decent living. You are also among the 101 economists who recently supported an increase in the minimum wage from $4.25 an hour to $5.15. Some may view these as contradictory positions. Can you explain these views?

TOBIN: The minimum wage has fallen a lot in real terms—way below what it was about 10 years ago. I thought this time that not much is being done for poor, low-wage working people in the present political climate. Public assistance, food stamps, welfare, Medicaid and other social programs are all under attack. The minimum wage always had to be recognized as having good income consequences—a number of people get higher wages. So, I thought in this instance those advantages outweighed the small loss of jobs.

And then there were these studies by Krueger and Card which I think showed that the elasticity of employment relative to the minimum wage is pretty small—they couldn't find it at all. I know that's controversial and there are opposing studies, but the difference didn't seem like a big deal in terms of employment.

QUESTION: Even at a rate of $5.15 the minimum wage is below what it probably should be in real terms. Should it have been raised even higher? In other words, if you could wave a magic wand . . .

TOBIN: Oh, I don't know what the right number is, if any. I think I would prefer a much more generous permanent earned income tax credit—suitably more generous, and I would pursue my recommendations of years ago for a negative income tax. We're not doing any of those things and we're not likely to do any of those things. I can't believe that the minimum wage is such a big deal and that it is such an important matter to conservative economists. There are a lot more important issues upon us in this country than that one.

QUESTION: Have you given much thought to the Social Security issue—any proposals?

TOBIN: Oh yes, I have given it some thought, and there's no way of getting around the fact that to have an actuarially sound old-age retirement system—Social Security—we need to have some combination of reducing benefits or raising the payroll taxes. I do think that moving gradually in the direction of converting some part of the Social Security system—for workers who are now young—into a defined contribution plan would be a good idea. And then possibly investing some of the trust fund that is produced in a defined contribution plan in equities, that would be a good idea, too. I'm not in favor, however, of giving people back their payroll taxes and letting them invest in whatever they want to. I'm not in favor of that—privatization in that sense. I think that would be a madhouse and I hesitate to imagine the competition of bond and stock salesmen for every old geezer's Social Security fund.

It's not out of the question to fix up the system for the next, say, 75 years, which is the usual horizon in which the Social Security plans are made. Now the question is how to do that by some changes in the structure of benefits and taxes; for example, raising the age of retirement—one might want to raise that by indexing it, formally or informally, to longevity. There's no reason that 65 should be the normal age of retirement. In the past, that meant 10 more years of life and now it means 20.

Reflections of a Central Banker*

ALAN BLINDER

I am here today in a very new role for me. While I am not young by any reasonable criterion, I am very young as a central banker. I've been here at the Kansas City Fed conferences in Jackson Hole several times before, but always as an academic speaker, where my role was clearly to say something and maybe even to say something interesting. It is quite clear that, in my new job, my new role is to say nothing and certainly not to say anything interesting.

Mindful of that dictum, I'd like to take us back to the perspective of a central banker, which is to say back to macroeconomics—a subject we haven't talked about very much in the symposium in general, but especially not this morning. (That is not criticism at all; I feel it was quite appropriate to discuss the things we have discussed this morning.) In particular, I was very glad to see, when I received the program, that this is a conference about *reducing*, not *increasing*, unemployment. Charts 1 and 2 (eight panels in all) illustrate what a woman from Mars who landed here in Jackson Hole to look at the unemployment history of the world since 1970 would have seen: the standardized (by the Organization for Economic Cooperation and Development [OECD]) unemployment rates of a nonrandomly se-

*This is an excerpt from a paper presented at a symposium at Jackson Hole, Wyoming, on August 27, 1994. Alan Blinder, now professor of economics at Princeton University, was then vice-chairman of the Board of Governors of the Federal Reserve System.

CHART 1 Standardized Unemployment Rates

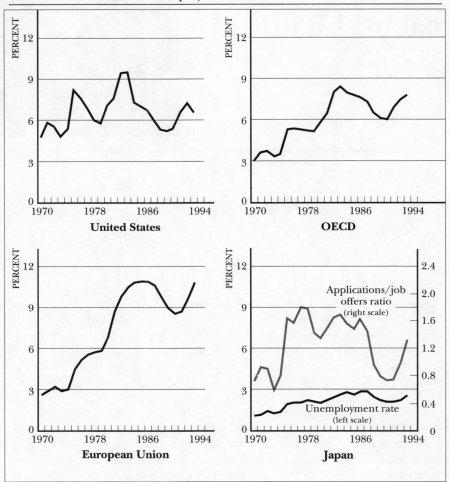

Sources: OECD Main Economic Indicators.

lected sample. The eight panels cover every country represented on the program—including the OECD and the European Union as countries—except, I'm sorry to say, New Zealand. That's because the OECD does not have a standardized unemployment rate for New Zealand that goes back this far. So this is the entire available sample. The hypothetical woman from Mars could be forgiven for wondering if the governments of these countries were really worrying about *reducing* unemployment during this

CHART 2 Standardized Unemployment Rates

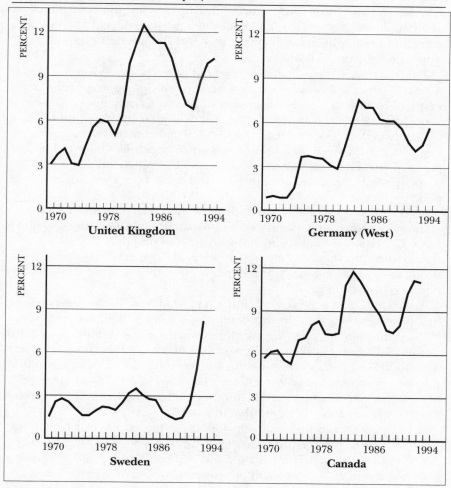

Sources: OECD Main Economic Indicators.

period rather than *increasing* unemployment. If they were worrying about reducing it, they weren't doing too well—except perhaps for Japan and the United States.

Now, in my view, central banks, or more generally macroeconomic policies, do indeed have a role in reducing unemployment as well as, not incidentally, in reducing inflation. Before I pursue that point further, there is a preliminary point—actually a hurdle which, if not jumped, leaves nothing more to say on the subject. That hurdle is this: for a central bank to have any role in either raising or reducing unemployment, you have to believe in Keynesianism. If you don't, changes in aggregate demand are all dissipated in prices right away—up or down—and you just don't have any ability to affect the unemployment rate.

The *Fortune Encyclopedia of Economics* has a definition of Keynesian economics. I wrote it, so I know what's in it. I am only going to summarize the first half of it, which is the definition of *positive* Keynesianism, forgetting about any *normative* considerations. This definition has three pieces, and I'll just read them briefly. First, it says: "A Keynesian believes that aggregate demand is influenced by a host of economic decisions—both public and private—and sometimes behaves erratically. The public decisions include, most prominently, those on monetary and fiscal (i.e., spending and tax) policy."

Second, it says that a Keynesian believes that: ". . . changes in aggregate demand, whether anticipated or unanticipated, have their greatest short-run impact on real output and employment, not on prices."

And third: "Keynesians believe that prices and, especially, wages respond slowly to changes in supply and demand, resulting in shortages and surpluses, especially of labor."

That is at least one person's definition of what it means to be Keynesian, in a positive sense. Now, by this definition, I submit that President Nixon had it right when he said, "We are all Keynesians now." (I think he said this in the 1970s.) Money is not neutral, and I don't think I have to take any time to defend that proposition any longer—although I must say that, if this were a conference of academics, I probably would. If you accept this proposition, then I can go on. If you don't, of course, I can sit down right now. (I suppose I shouldn't put that to a vote!)

If you accept this proposition and you accept the natural rate hypothesis, which has been thoroughly discussed at this meeting, they lead to what I like to call "the approximate dichotomy." I'll come at the end to why it is only "approximate"—or at least one reason why—but this is what I mean by the approximate dichotomy: where employment is concerned, in the short run macroeconomics is everything and in the long run macroeconomics is nothing.

Let me elaborate slightly on what I mean by that. In the short run, changes in aggregate demand can and do easily change the unemployment rate by, say, plus or minus two percentage points. Such events happen frequently in business cycles. There is nothing, I submit, that we know in the way of microeconomic interventions that could have an effect remotely close to that in the United States—certainly not in the short run, and maybe not even in the long run. So that's one-half of the dichotomy.

However, in the long run the meaning of the natural rate hypothesis, as Dale Mortensen stated clearly this morning, is that the unemployment rate will converge to the natural rate *regardless of macroeconomic policy*. And that means, roughly speaking, that the employment rate of five to ten years from now has nothing to do with today's macroeconomic policy. The latter is totally irrelevant. Today's macroeconomic policy will, however, have something to do with the price level of five to ten years from now.

I emphasize this dichotomy because, while it is mother's milk to economists, it is almost totally unknown outside the economics profession—indeed it is a totally foreign doctrine. Very few people have in their heads the notion that the effects of aggregate demand on jobs are temporary, which is not to say ephemeral—I don't mean they are gone in three to six months, they are certainly not—but temporary. Nor do most people realize that a very big microeconomic achievement, at least in the United States, might be reducing the natural rate of unemployment by 0.25 percent. That would be a major, major achievement. But I think that very few people outside the economics profession understand either part of this dichotomy, which is a shame.

In view of this approximate dichotomy, what is a poor central banker to do? My view is that we should remember a television quiz show that I occasionally watched in my wasted youth called *The Price Is Right*. You may remember that on *The Price Is Right* an object would appear, and contestants were supposed to guess the price. You won if you came as close to the actual price as possible *without going over*. That was the name of the game. Similarly, in my view, the job of a central bank, in this regard, is to guide the employment rate up to its natural rate, but not higher than that. By that criterion, I think the United States is extremely close to being "on target," but the European Union, I believe, is quite far from being on target.

I have stated quite clearly, I think, that I believe the central bank does have a role in reducing unemployment, or raising employment. But, as we know, not all central banks explicitly recognize an employment objective of that sort. We heard very eloquently at lunch yesterday, from Mr. Brash, the virtues of single-minded concentration on an inflation, or a price level, objective. The charge given by the Congress to the Federal Reserve is quite different, as many of you know. It calls upon us to pursue *both* maximum employment *and* stable prices. Since these two objectives conflict in the short run, the Federal Reserve Act calls upon us to strike a balance. That has always seemed very appropriate to me.

In thinking about the fact that different central banks have quite different stated objectives, I started to wonder whether the objectives actually matter. And, while I was wondering about that, I stumbled upon something which some of you have seen before: a ranking of central banks by Alex Cukierman and two coauthors. (See Chart 3.) Cukierman *et al.* rated 21 industrial countries by what they called "central bank independence." Actually, I think this was quite a big misnomer because, if you notice, the United States is ranked pretty low. And I can tell you we feel fairly independent at the Fed, at least inside the building. In fact, the rankings really rate central banks on the singlemindedness of their concentration on inflation reduction, or price-level stability. Here, again, I must apologize to New Zealand. I didn't make up these rankings, and they came before the Reserve Bank Act of 1989. New Zealand, among other countries, would clearly be ranked differently today.

What I've done in Chart 3 is looked at the period of disinflation: 1980–1993. It seems to me that around 1980 the countries of the industrialized world looked back at the 1970s and said: "Enough—indeed, too much. We had an awful lot of inflation, it didn't do anybody any good, and we ought to get rid of it." There was a kind of sea change in attitudes around the world, although not with exactly the same timing everywhere.

So Chart 3 examines the period between 1980 and 1993. Central banks are ranked by the objective index created by Cukierman *et al.*, with 1.0 connoting the most single-minded concentration on inflation reduction—you see, for example, that the Bundesbank is on the far right on this criterion—and with zero on the other extreme: banks that did not have any inflation objective at all in their charge (that includes the Bank of Japan and it included then, but not now, the Bank of France). And the question I asked was: Did the bank's legally stated objective make any difference to what happened in this 13-year period? Was there any systematic difference between the banks that were focused on inflation reduction and those that were not?

Well, the top panel shows the changes in inflation over that period. You can see that it is negative for every one of these countries; this was, after all, a period of disinflation. But the answer to the question is no. There is no correlation . . . between how much inflation fell and the legal charge of the central bank.

The lower panel shows that there was some correlation—not overwhelming, but noticeable—between the rise in unemployment and the central bank's objective. . . . So unemployment rose in every one of these countries, essentially; and it rose more in the countries whose central banks were more singlemindedly devoted to inflation reduction. But the difference is not tremendously significant. The message, I think, may be that the significance of the central bank's charge may be more apparent than real. But I wouldn't dismiss it entirely. Now, there is a two-handed answer for you!

CHART 3 Central Bank Objectives, Inflation, and Unemployment

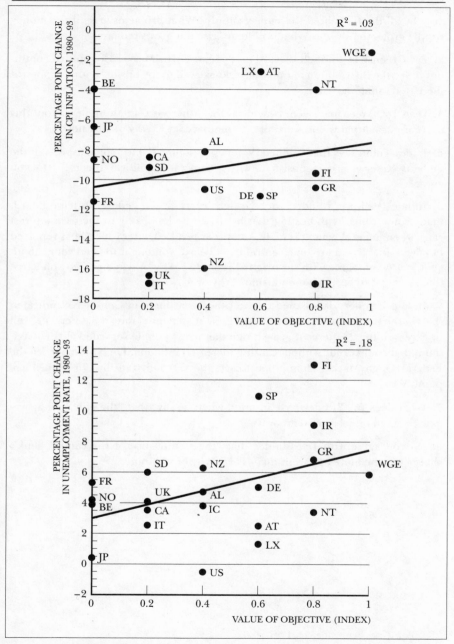

Source: A. Cukierman, S. Webb, and B. Neyapti, "Measuring the Independence of Central Banks and Its Effect on Policy Outcomes," *World Bank Economic Review* 6, 3 (September 1992) 353–398.

QUESTIONS FOR ANALYSIS

1. Why all the fuss about the money supply? What problems arise if the money supply grows too slowly? What problems arise if it grows too fast?

2. Dr. Greenspan testified that: "The Federal Open Market Committee continues to see the distribution of inflation risks skewed to the upside"—that is, toward increased inflation. Why?

3. Does Dr. Greenspan seem convinced that "there is something new about this current period that would warrant . . . complacency?" Why or why not?

4. James Tobin says that "monetary policy is politics," and "some aspects of the Federal Reserve are inconsistent with democratic political theory." Do you agree?

5. In late 1994, Dr. Blinder, then vice-chairman of the Federal Reserve Board, made some remarks indicating that he would be less likely to increase interest rates when unemployment is high. An uproar resulted, after which he is reported to have said, "If you are on a central bank board, you ought to keep your mouth shut."* Do you agree with his original remarks? Why or why not? Do you agree that he ought to keep his mouth shut? Why or why not?

6. In late October, data issued by the U.S. Department of Commerce indicated that, in the third quarter of 1994, GDP grew at an annual rate of 3.4 percent, well in excess of the 2.5 percent growth rate that many people regarded as the maximum that could occur without causing increased inflation. On November 15, the Federal Open Market Committee raised the discount rate by .75 percentage point. Why?

7. What does Dr. Blinder have in mind when he says that "the effects of aggregate demand on jobs are temporary"?

8. Do you agree with Dr. Blinder that "the significance of the central bank's charge may be more apparent than real"? Why or why not?

*New York Times, September 11, 1994, p. 2F.

PART ELEVEN

INTER-
NATIONAL
TRADE
POLICY

The mid-1990s have seen a great deal of controversy over U.S. trade policy. Some influential political leaders and industrialists feel strongly that we should engage in "managed trade"; others disagree—equally strongly. The first article is by Paul Krugman of Massachusetts Institute of Technology who argues that the alleged competitiveness problem of the United States is greatly exaggerated. The second article is by Robert A. Lutz, president of the Chrysler Corporation, who favors managed trade. The third article is by Robert T. Parry, president of the Federal Reserve Bank of San Francisco, who opposes managed trade.

The Fixation on Competitiveness*

PAUL KRUGMAN

In the movie *The Music Man,* Robert Preston plays a traveling salesman who specializes in selling musical instruments and uniforms for marching bands to small towns. To make his sale in River City, he needs to convince local leaders that they have a problem he can solve. And so he manages to turn the formerly innocuous pool hall into a symbol of gathering social danger, to which the answer is, of course, the healthy town spirit that only a properly equipped school band can provide.

Many policy entrepreneurs (and to be honest, not a few professors) play a similar game. They have a solution; now they have to convince the politicians and the public that there is an appropriate problem. Often they fail: despite his best efforts, Robert Bartley of *The Wall Street Journal* never managed to convince many people that monetary chaos looms unless we put America back on the gold standard. Sometimes, however, policy entrepreneurs and the politicians who make alliance with them are spectacularly successful at creating imagined problems to which their favorite policy prescriptions are the answer.

The imaginary problem that galvanized the supply-siders and Ronald Reagan was the danger of Big Government: a government that taxed people too much, then wasted the money on legions of useless bureaucrats and

*This is an excerpt from Paul Krugman, *Peddling Prosperity* (New York: W. W. Norton, 1994). Paul Krugman is professor of economics at Massachusetts Institute of Technology.

generous welfare handouts to the undeserving poor. Big Government is not, of course, wholly imaginary. Taxes *are* a significant burden on all of us, and there are indeed useless bureaucrats and undeserving welfare recipients. But as a diagnosis of what was wrong with the American economy, it was deeply misleading; and the myth of Big Government both distracted America from coming to grips with its real problems and created new difficulties.

The supply-siders have now retreated to their think tanks, though they still hope to return for revenge. For the time being, Big Government is no longer an effective slogan, and middle-class Americans are angrier at the undeserving rich than the undeserving poor. But the policy entrepreneurs now riding high have convinced many Americans that we have a new kind of trouble in River City: trouble with a capital "C" that stands for "Competitiveness."

The strategic traders have now sold the American public (and for the most part themselves, for only a few policy entrepreneurs are entirely cynical) on the idea that our most crucial economic problem is our struggle with other advanced nations for global markets. The subtitle of Lester Thurow's *Head to Head* is "The Coming Economic Battle Among Japan, Europe, and America"; the jacket entices readers by saying, "The most decisive war of the century is being waged right now . . . and we may have already decided to lose."

Unfortunately, the alleged competitive problem of the United States is as much a fantasy as Reagan's myth of wasteful Big Government. The United States has some real problems in international competition, just as it really has some unproductive bureaucrats and welfare cheats. But in the image it conveys of what's really wrong with the economy, Clinton's rhetoric is as far off as Reagan's.

Economic rhetoric based on the myth of international competition as war has some advantages. It is easier to mobilize voters to support painful policies like tax increases and cuts in popular programs by claiming that the goal is national security—and President Clinton did just that in his highly effective 1993 State of the Union address. But ultimately the rhetoric of competitiveness will be destructive, because it can all too easily lead both to bad policies and to a neglect of the real issues.

The rise of the strategic traders poses two main risks. One is that in their effort to win global markets, they will destroy them instead. The other is that the commitment to a foolish ideology in one area will undermine economic policy across the board.

THE RISK OF TRADE WAR

There are two kinds of trade war: the imaginary ones that protectionists and strategic traders claim we are fighting all the time, and the real ones that happen when they get their way.

The fantasy of the strategic traders is that international trade is by its nature international competition—that countries that trade with each other are in a struggle over who gets the spoils. In reality there is almost nothing to this view: what a country gets depends almost entirely on its own performance, and there is nothing competitive about it. But when countries *believe* that they are in a competitive struggle, or when they become captive to the special interests that benefit from trade conflict, they can fall into what is generally known as a trade war.

A trade war in which countries restrict each other's exports in pursuit of some illusory advantage is not much like a real war. On one hand, nobody gets killed. On the other, unlike real wars, it is almost impossible for anyone to win, since the main losers when a country imposes barriers to trade are not foreign exporters but domestic residents. In effect, a trade war is a conflict in which each country uses most of its ammunition to shoot itself in the foot.

And yet once a trade war is started, it can be very difficult to stop. Each country finds it politically impossible to free up its trade without corresponding "concessions" from other countries, and these may be very hard to negotiate. In other words, once the world has gotten caught up in a wave of tit-for-tat protectionism, it can take decades to undo the damage.

Consider the lessons of the interwar period. A trade war among the advanced countries erupted after the United States passed the infamous Smoot-Hawley tariff in 1929, and intensified as countries made desperate efforts to find ways out of the Great Depression. Yet most people, even including the senators who voted for Smoot-Hawley, soon realized that protectionism had gone too far. The United States began trying to negotiate tariffs down again as early as 1934, and after World War II both the political and the economic environment were very favorable for trade liberalization. Once the global trading system had been shattered, however, it was very hard to put back together; trade among industrial countries didn't regain its 1914 level until 1970.

In the 1990s, the world is ripe for another outbreak of trade war. The key economic ingredients that led to protectionism in the interwar period—slow growth, persistent high unemployment—are back again, especially in Europe. Meanwhile, the political strengths that helped make the freeing up of trade after World War II possible—a strong leading nation and a common purpose—are gone with the relative decline of the United States and the end of the Cold War. It wouldn't take much miscalculation to start a round of tariffs, countertariffs, and mutual recrimination that could repeat the interwar experience of shrinking trade.

Would this be a catastrophe? No, but it would add significantly to our problems. Big, largely self-contained economies like the United States, the European Community, and Japan could take restricted global trade in stride. Even a quite nasty trade war would reduce their real income only a percentage point or two. But smaller countries, more dependent on world markets to help them make up for the small size of their internal markets and their limited resources, would either have to scramble to form commercial alliances with the big players or be left dangerously out in the cold. It would not be surprising if a world of trade conflict among the big advanced countries was a world of political instability, and maybe growing anti-Western feeling, in smaller and poorer countries from Latin America to the former Soviet Republics.

World trade, then, is in an endangered state, in which we could easily stumble into an era of trade conflict that would be at least as hard to get rid of as Ronald Reagan's deficit. Yet it is at this of all moments that strategic traders in the United States think that we need to get tough with other countries in pursuit of "competitiveness."

Imagine the following scenario: Clinton administration officials—ignoring advice from conventional economists—decide that Japan's trade surplus is the root of many of America's economic difficulties, and decide to demand that Japan not only take measures to reduce that surplus but agree to meet specific numerical targets. The Japanese are indignant: they point out, correctly, that it is perfectly reasonable for a country with a very high savings rate to invest a significant fraction of those savings abroad, and that Japan's trade surplus is simply the other side of its capital account deficit. Besides, they say, what are they supposed to do—run huge budget deficits to soak up all that private saving?

The strategic traders in the Clinton administration nonetheless present their demands at an economic summit—and the Japanese reject them. At this point the U.S. government faces a dilemma. To drop the issue would look like weakness; but there is no real policy option other than to close U.S. markets to Japanese goods. And so protectionism it is—a protectionism that is matched by Japanese retaliation and European emulation. Within two years the results of four decades of negotiations to open world markets are reversed.

An unlikely scenario? At the time of writing, much of it had already happened. The Treasury Department is usually a bastion of free trade thinking, but in May 1993 Lawrence Summers, now the Undersecretary of the Treasury for International Affairs, asserted in a speech that "Japan's surplus is the major asymmetry in the global economy" and that this surplus was a "significant drag on global growth"; he followed this assertion with the statement that "The United States will focus less on process and more on results, and results have to be measurable." Everyone knew what he meant: the U.S. Trade Representative had for several weeks been telling reporters that the United States was likely to demand that Japan impose a ceiling on its trade surplus at the next meeting of the Group of Seven industrial countries. Meanwhile, Japanese officials and the Japanese public were furious and defiant in the face of American pressure.

One hopes that by the time this book is published this particular scenario will turn out to have been a premature alarm. As long as the administration is committed to the ideology of strategic trade, however, the risk of trade war will remain high.

So the direct threat from the ascendancy of strategic traders is that their fixation on the supposed problem of competitiveness will set off a trade war. Like the budget deficit created by the supply-siders, a trade war will not destroy the U.S. economy; but also like the budget deficit, it will be very hard to get rid of.

Managed Trade*

ROBERT A. LUTZ

Thank you, Dean Hasler. And good morning to all of you. It's great to be back here at my alma mater. I have a lot of fond memories of Berkeley, starting with the fact that I got a terrific education here from an absolutely brilliant faculty.

I also remember that going to school here—back in those, the earliest days of the Free Speech Movement—was a real lesson in *character-building* for me. You see, I'd already been in the Marine Corps before I started school, and, while in school, I continued as a First Lieutenant in the reserves.

And, since I had a crew cut, an affinity for the military, and wrote letters to the "Daily Californian," I sort of became the resident right-wing speaker at a host of panel discussions around campus. The Free-Speech types didn't want to appear biased, so they put this obviously wacko, lunatic-fringe conservative on their panels just to sort of even things out.

The funny thing, however, is that I was actually a *moderate!* I just *looked* conservative by comparison!

And I must say, it's good to see that things haven't changed much here. I read recently about how you had a student who was coming to class in the nude—"The Naked Guy," I believe he was called? I especially liked it when,

*This speech was delivered at the Haas School of Business Faculty–Alumni Colloquium, University of California at Berkeley, on April 24, 1993. Robert A. Lutz is president of the Chrysler Corporation.

after he got expelled, he said, "My original plan was that I was going to get expelled and then sue for readmittance. *I can learn a lot suing them.*"

Now, I've heard of "independent study," but I think that's a little *ridiculous*—even for Berkeley!

Anyway, it's great to be back here. And I'd like to begin by commending you for choosing a quote-unquote "global focus" for your discussions here at this colloquium today. It's become a cliche, of course, but the business world today truly *is* a global world.

And we in the auto business perhaps know that better than most. Ever since the two oil shocks of the 1970s gave foreign automakers (most notably the Japanese) their first real toehold in this market, we in Detroit have had to struggle with the realities of tough international competition coming at us each and every day right here in our own back yard.

And, though it wasn't always easy, we've learned a lot from that experience.

We've learned, for instance, that over time there's been a certain convergence in consumer tastes around the world. No longer do you have the stereotype of Americans driving nothing but land yachts, Japanese driving nothing but minicars, and Europeans driving spartan econocars. Today, cars like, say, the Honda Accord, the Ford Taurus, or like my company's new Chrysler Concorde, Dodge Intrepid, and Eagle Vision sedans fit in virtually anywhere in the world.

We've also learned that you can run, but you can't hide, when it comes to dealing with international competition. In fact, I daresay that any company today that is still benchmarking just—or even *primarily*—its domestic competitors is probably doomed to failure.

And finally, we've learned that nothing is forever—that, with hard work, even the most seemingly permanent of trends can indeed be turned around. Case in point: In the past 15 months, Chrysler has gained more than two points of total market share in the U.S. And in that same period, the Japanese automakers as a whole have *lost* five-and-a-half points of share. That, I submit, is a *sea change* if there ever was one!

But for all that globalization and international competition has taught us in recent years, we have also learned that global trade has a dark side—a *very* dark side. And that dark side is that not all countries in the world play by the same rules when it comes to international trade.

Oh, sure, everybody pays homage to the GATT, and everybody professes to be "free traders." But, in reality, most everybody in the world—with the notable exception of the United States—practices something that has come to be known as "*managed* trade."

And that's a fact, I know, that the head of President Clinton's Council of Economic Advisers, Berkeley's own Laura D'Andrea Tyson, has herself pointed out many times. The term I believe she likes to use is "aggressive unilateralism." That is, the United States shouldn't be afraid to act *aggressively* and *unilaterally* (if need be) in demanding trade agreements that would, in fact, help *increase* world trade. In other words, in the face of managed trade, we shouldn't be afraid to practice a little managed trade ourselves.

Now, I know that Professor Tyson and others in the Clinton Administration have taken a lot of heat for their views. For example, in the *New York Times* last month, Jagdish Bhagwati of Columbia University said, "This should be the spring of hope, and instead we might get nuclear winter."

Which brings me to the (I hope) rather catchy title of my talk here today: "Managed Trade: Spring of Hope or Nuclear Winter?" In other words: Should managed trade be a part of this country's economic strategy in the context of today's global economy—part of, if you will, our "spring of hope," especially as we strive for some long-overdue economic revitalization?

Or is it, as Professor Bhagwati suggests, a step down a slippery slope leading to a 1930s-style trade war and to a sort of economic nuclear winter?

That's the central question that I'd like to address here today. And by way of illustration, I'd like to use some examples from the auto industry—not just because I know it best, but because the auto industry—the good ol' "smokestack," "sunset" auto industry—is shaping up to be one of *the* prime battlegrounds for global trade issues today. As President Clinton's Trade Representative, Mickey Kantor, put it recently, Detroit is at "the *nerve center* of America's new trade and economic dialogue."

Why? Well, because autos and auto parts have accounted for more than *two-thirds* of America's absolutely staggering $450-*billion*-dollar trade deficit with Japan over the past decade. Obviously, therefore, our *overall* trade deficit cannot come down unless the *auto* deficit is attacked.

Let me tell a story that's been very much in the news lately and which, I think, pretty well symbolizes our whole auto trade with Japan. It's the story of multipurpose vehicles, or "MPVs" for short. An MPV is a vehicle like, say, the Toyota 4-Runner sport utility.

A funny thing happens to a 4-Runner when it's imported into this country. Four U.S. regulators all look it over. The fellow from the Environmental Protection Agency inspects it and declares that it is "a truck," and will therefore only have to meet the emissions standards for U.S. trucks, which are not as strict as those for cars.

Behind him is the man from the National Highway Traffic Safety Administration, who certifies that it is indeed a truck so it won't have to have the same safety devices as a car.

And then comes the inspector from the Department of Transportation, who also agrees that the vehicle is a truck so it won't have to meet the higher fuel economy requirements of a car.

But then comes the fourth inspector. He's from the U.S. Customs Service. He looks at the 4-Runner and says, "Nope, this isn't a truck at all; it's a *car!*" And that means it pays a duty of only 2.5 percent instead of the 25 percent duty on trucks.

Now, what's going on here? Well, back in February of 1989, after intense lobbying by Japanese automakers, the U.S. Treasury Department, in a virtually unprecedented decision, overruled its own Customs Service and reclassified Japanese sport utilities and minivans from trucks to cars. It was, as President Clinton himself put it in a press conference last month, a "$300-million-dollar-a-year freebie to the Japanese for no apparent reason."

Now, maybe it wouldn't have been so bad if the U.S. had gotten some trade concessions *of its own* in return. But we got absolutely *nothing*. Now, I daresay that if a business student here at the Haas School suggested such an obviously win-*lose* deal as a solution to a case study, he'd be joining "The Naked Guy" out on the street!

But that's not the only trade issue related to autos that's been in the news lately. The other one is *dumping*.

As you may know, earlier this year General Motors, Ford, and Chrysler had contemplated filing a dumping charge against Japanese automakers. We had, quite frankly, what we considered to be a *very* strong case. (And it applied, by the way, to *all* major Japanese automakers, across *all* segments of the market—from small cars to luxury cars. And we're talking about cars being dumped for as much as *$5,000* below their prices in Japan. So, this was no inconsequential matter.)

But we backed off—at least for now—in part to give the Clinton Administration a chance to try to solve the problem, and in part, again quite frankly, because of the well-orchestrated negative PR campaign that we were already beginning to experience for even *thinking* about filing a charge.

Now, in concert with that high-priced PR campaign, the Japanese automakers, of course, swore up and down that they were *not* dumping. However, they've nonetheless quietly been raising their prices in recent months (even *before* the yen started to rise)—which might, I think, lead a cynic to believe that just maybe they'd rather pocket the money themselves than have the U.S. government get it in added tariffs!

Meanwhile, amid all the PR and all of the mud-slinging, a couple of simple things seemed to have gotten lost: One is that dumping is *against the law*—against both U.S. *and* international trade law. And Japan certainly knows that as well as anybody, given that they just recently imposed anti-dumping duties of *their own*—on manganese coming in from China!

The other thing that seems to have gotten lost is that "managed trade" is really *already* being practiced here in the United States—only it's all too often the *Japanese,* and not us, who are managing it!

Now, at this point, I know that perhaps some of you might be inclined to say, "Hey, why don't you guys in Detroit quit whining, and just shut up and compete?"

Well, we *are* competing. Earlier, I mentioned the market share that we at Chrysler have won back here in the U.S. We've also, by the way, been doing quite well in Europe. From a virtual standstill, we've sold more than 200,000 vehicles in Europe in the last four years. And so far *this* year, our European sales are *up* 30 percent, while the market as a whole is *down* 17 percent.

But the one place where we continue to have very little success at all is—you guessed it—*Japan.*

And it's not just us—*no* foreign automakers really have had any success to speak of in Japan. In fact, total import penetration in the Japanese auto market was less than *three* percent last year. By contrast, the Japanese have routinely taken up to *ten times* that amount of the U.S. market (and here in California, of course, it's been more like *15* times).

Now, why is that? Well, let me cite the case of Chrysler's new Jeep Grand Cherokee sport utility (which, by the way, competes head to head with the Toyota 4-Runner). The Grand Cherokee is, by any measure, a world-class vehicle. It won Motor Trend's "Truck of the Year" award last year. And it's completely sold out both here in the United States and in Europe.

Yet we have a tough time selling Grand Cherokees *in Japan.* And no wonder, given that they cost over $15,000 *more* in Japan than they do here!

That's because the Japanese won't accept our certifications, because everything has to be inspected, and mostly because of the maze of red tape and gargantuan distribution costs associated with Japan's notoriously closed distribution system.

And "closed" it is. In fact, until just recently, Japanese automakers prevented their dealers in Japan from selling any imported cars at all!

Now, if we did this in the U.S., of course, we'd be thrown in jail for violating antitrust laws. But in Japan, it's been standard practice. And, as a result, while foreign cars are sold today at more than *90* percent of all dealerships in the United States, foreign cars are sold at just *seven* percent of all dealerships in Japan!

But, of course, it's not just cars that have been kept out of Japan. The list of products is, in my view, embarrassingly long. And, of course, as the folks down in Silicon Valley know all too well, that list includes *computer chips.*

Now, I understand that trade tensions eased a bit out here recently when it was announced that, in the fourth quarter, U.S. and other foreign semiconductor makers had finally—*finally*—achieved the target of 20 percent of the Japanese chip market. But I think it's worth keeping in mind *how* our chip makers actually achieved that goal.

The process began way back in 1985, when the Reagan Administration (of all people!) accepted an anti-dumping case and a "Super 301" unfair trade case brought against the Japanese. That "chip shot," as it was called, then eventually led to negotiations, which, in turn, produced the 20-percent import target. (And I understand, by the way, that that 20-percent figure is still less than *half* the market share that U.S. chip makers enjoy *elsewhere* in the world. And it's also almost identical to the share of the *U.S.* chip market that *Japanese* companies enjoy!)

Anyway, the upshot is that in the case of computer chips the U.S. followed a policy of, yes, *managed trade*. In fact, it was one that definitely contained some Laura Tyson-style "aggressive unilateralism." And, lo and behold, it's *working*!

Now, I know that Professor Tyson along with others in the Administration, such as Mickey Kantor, have been called "trade agnostics" for their pragmatic, results-oriented approach to global trade. And I'm sure those who say that often mean it in a derogatory sense—that Tyson and Kantor and others have somehow lost their ideological souls.

But I, for one, think there's a big difference between being a trade *atheist* (that is, somebody who *has* lost his soul and given up on free trade altogether) and a trade *agnostic*. A trade agnostic, it seems to me, is someone who believes that real free trade could indeed exist in the world someday— but who in the meantime speaks softly and carries a big stick!

By that definition, the *Europeans,* to name just one example, are certainly trade agnostics. Last year—as part of the "EC '92" negotiations—the European Community told Japanese automakers that they can have no more than *16 percent* of the European auto market through the end of this century. (That compares, despite their recent losses, to the *24*-percent share of the market that the Japanese have in the *U.S.* today.)

Now, I know that Professor Tyson herself might even say that an industry like autos is too mature, and too "low-tech," to qualify for the benefits of managed trade here in this country.

But, for starters, we're hardly low-tech. You may not know this, but the auto industry buys *20 percent*—that's *one in five*—of all the semiconductors sold in this country. In fact, a car today with an air bag, ABS brakes, and traction control has the computing power of the on-board guidance system of the Apollo moonshot!

(And, by the way, I think that Silicon Valley should be more than a little dismayed by reports recently that while U.S. chip makers supply *60* percent of the chips that go into luxury cars worldwide—the kind of cars most likely *to have* traction control and that other high-tech stuff—their market share of the Japanese luxury brands Lexus and Infiniti is just *seven* percent!)

And as far as being a so-called "mature" industry goes—yes, the auto industry is guilty of being mature. But the fact is, every industry in this country *aspires* to be mature one day. We *all* want to perpetuate ourselves. But think about this: If we allow *today's* high-employment, high-value-added, mature industries to become victims of *somebody else's* managed-trade policies, than what does that bode for the mature industries of *tomorrow?*

Going back to Europe, the Europeans have basically said that their key, strategic industries, including autos, and the jobs that they represent are *important* to them. Now, maybe in the case of Airbus and agricultural subsidies, they've gone overboard a little bit! But by and large, they have, in my opinion, found a much better trade-off than we have between the so-called "rights of the consumer" and *also*-very-legitimate rights of those very same citizens to be gainfully employed.

Which makes sense. After all, if you think about it, the most useless consumer of all is one *without a job!*

For some reason, we haven't seemed quite ready to grasp that reality here in this country. Although in this so-called "jobless recovery" of ours, and with all of the so-called "hollowing-out" of American industry that's taken place over the last decade or so (including the layoffs at IBM and elsewhere in high tech), I think maybe we're *beginning* to understand.

And I also think that we're finally beginning to understand that our trade policies (or lack thereof) have definitely played a *key role* in that hollowing-out and in that joblessness.

So, to get back to my central question—"Managed Trade: Spring of Hope or Nuclear Winter?"—I think, in truth, that we are actually experiencing a bit of "nuclear winter" *right now!* (Or maybe you might call it *"neutron* winter"—the buildings are still standing, it's just the *jobs* that are gone!)

I also think that if we want to get this economy moving strongly forward again, and *keep* it moving forward as a global leader into the 21st century, then there's no doubt that a more pragmatic—indeed, one might say a more *realistic*—trade policy needs to be adopted. *That,* in my opinion, is our "spring of hope."

And if that sounds like "trade agnosticism," then so be it. But in my book, it makes a whole lot more sense to be an agnostic on this subject than a so-called "true believer" who keeps waiting for his savior . . . but in the meantime winds up getting crucified *himself!*

And on that note, I'd like to thank you for letting this "prodigal-son-of-Berkeley-turned-trade-agnostic" return to his alma mater to offer his I-hope-not-*too*-blasphemous opinions.

If nothing else, it's nice knowing, all these years later, that I'm probably no longer the resident conservative here on campus!

Thank you very much.

U.S. Trade Deficits and International Competitiveness*

ROBERT T. PARRY

hank you. It's a pleasure to be here. Today I'd like to talk about our trade deficit and what it implies about our ability to compete globally. We've had this trade deficit for over a decade. Some people, and a number of policymakers, see this as a symptom that we've lost our edge in international competition. Here's their diagnosis of the problem: Foreign competitors are able to take markets away from U.S. producers because they have some important advantages. In particular, they have lower wages, superior technology, and "unfair" trade practices.

What's their prescription to fix the problem and return U.S. industries to competitive health? They'd like to see the government try to manage international competition by taking a more protectionist stance and targeting certain industries for special support.

My own view is that this analysis is off the mark. I do *not* think the trade deficit is due to lower wages, superior technology, and "unfair" trade practices abroad. On the contrary, I think we can find the sources of the trade deficit in certain macroeconomic fundamentals—namely, our own government budget deficit and our investment and saving patterns. Moreover, I don't think the trade deficit is necessarily the best way to judge our com-

*This speech was delivered to the National Association of Business Economists in Chicago, Illinois, on September 20, 1993. Robert T. Parry is president of the Federal Reserve Bank of San Francisco.

petitiveness. There are more important factors to consider. In particular, I would point to price competitiveness and productivity.

Let me begin by looking at just how bad the trade deficit is. First, I think it's a mistake to focus too much on the most recent numbers, which haven't been too good. The reason it's a mistake is that the source of the problem is more cyclical than it is structural. The U.S. has been in recovery for a while now. But many of our industrial trading partners are still in recession. So the recent bulge in our trade deficit is largely due to the fact that, as we continue to grow and import more, the weakness abroad is hurting our exports.

Now let me look at the longer view. Although the trade deficit has persisted for over a decade, the situation is much better now than it was in the mid-1980s. The merchandise trade deficit fell from a peak of $160 billion in 1987 to $96 billion in 1992. Relative to GDP, it declined from 3.5 percent to 1.6 percent. The current account deficit, which includes trade in services, improved even more dramatically. It dropped from a deficit of $167 billion in 1987 to $62 billion in 1992—or from 3.5 percent of GDP to 1 percent of GDP.

Why the turnaround? Because over the past six years, U.S. exports have surged. From 1986 through 1992 the total value of U.S. merchandise exports almost doubled, growing more than 12 percent per year. In volume terms, exports grew almost as fast, averaging more than 10 percent per year. A major source of strength in this export growth has been manufactures. And it's notable that this sector has continued to show strength even during the worldwide economic slowdown of the past few years. So the big picture on the trade deficit is that the situation is better than it was in the mid-1980s, because U.S. exports have surged since then.

Now let me look at the problem of "unfair trade practices." By this I mean such things as government support of selected industries through export subsidies and trade protection. The evidence is clear that virtually all countries, including the U.S., impose at least some restrictions on imports and provide government support for exports. Still, there's *no* evidence that the U.S. trade deficits of the 1980s were caused by greater foreign trade barriers or other unfair trade practices. First of all, between 1981 and 1987, when the deficit was at its peak, the deterioration in our trade position was *pervasive.* It spread uniformly and proportionately across capital goods, automotive products, and consumer goods. And the deterioration was roughly in proportion to each of our major trading partner's share of U.S. import and exports in 1981. If unfair foreign trade practices had caused the pervasive decline in the early 1980s, they would have had to change uniformly and suddenly around 1981, an unlikely conspiracy.

Of all the U.S. trading partners, Japan continues to be singled out for having the most unfair trading practices. But it's doubtful that such policies have been a major cause of U.S. trade deficits. First of all, the Japanese market has become somewhat more *open*—not more closed—over the past decade. Second, Japan's share of changes in the total U.S. non-oil merchandise trade deficit have been proportional to its U.S. trade share. For example, in 1981, about 9 percent of our exports went to Japan, and about 20 percent of our imports came from Japan. That left us with a bilateral deficit of $16 billion. If the same shares prevailed in 1992, we would have had a bilateral deficit of $57 billion—which is in fact a little larger than the actual deficit of $51 billion. So I think there's not much evidence to say that restrictive trade practices have been the driving force behind changes in the U.S. trade deficit.

Of course, the doors to Japanese and other foreign markets aren't exactly wide open to U.S. exporters. But even if existing foreign restrictions on U.S. exports were completely removed, most estimates suggest we'd reduce our trade deficit by only modest amounts.

Now let me look at our international competitiveness in terms of our production costs and productivity. Is there any evidence that U.S. price competitiveness declined during the 1980s? If we make the comparison in dollar terms, then the answer is: "Yes, price competitiveness *did* decline." Between 1980 and 1985 unit labor costs in dollars rose at an annual rate of 3.1 percent in the U.S., while unit labor costs fell in 10 of 11 other industrial countries.

But that information doesn't give us a complete picture. If we make the comparison in national currency terms, then unit labor costs actually *rose* in most of those other countries. Therefore, it was the appreciation of the dollar in the early 1980s, not underlying cost increases, that primarily caused U.S. manufacturers to lose price competitiveness to foreign producers during this period.

The fall of the dollar since the mid-1980s has made foreign unit labor costs measured in dollars now substantially higher than they were in 1980. Between the 1985 peak in the dollar and 1992, U.S. unit labor costs rose at only 1 percent per year, while costs in Japan, France, Germany, Korea, and Taiwan, for example, all rose at roughly 10 percent annually over the period 1985–1992. Therefore, most of the apparent improvement in U.S. international competitiveness is due to changes in the value of the dollar. Furthermore, manufacturing in the U.S. now appears to have a significant cost advantage over manufacturing in other countries.

What about productivity? The U.S. had relatively *strong* productivity growth during the 1980s. Between 1980 and 1985, manufacturers' output per worker grew 3.3 percent annually in the U.S., compared to 4.0 percent in Japan, 2.3 percent in France, and 2.1 percent in Germany. Since the mid-1980s U.S. productivity has continued to keep pace and even exceed that in much of the rest of the world. From 1985 to 1992 U.S. manufacturing output per worker grew at 2.9 percent per year, compared to 2.3 percent in Japan, 0.8 percent in Germany, and 2.8 percent in France.

Now that we can't blame the trade deficit on our competitors' lower labor costs, higher productivity, or unfair trade practices, where do we look for the source of it? The answer, I think, is in macroeconomic fundamentals. By definition, a country's trade balance is the mirror image of its pattern of saving and investment. So, for example, a country with more investment opportunities than its domestic saving can handle will borrow from abroad and run a trade deficit. This is true even if its costs are relatively low, its home markets are protected, and its exports are subsidized. The converse also holds true: A country with high saving relative to investment will run trade *surpluses*—even if its markets are open and its products are regarded as "noncompetitive."

In the case of the U.S., the emergence and persistence of large trade deficits since the early 1980s can be attributed largely to changes in the nation's saving-investment balance. Over the 1960s and 1970s, the U.S. (gross) national saving rate roughly equaled the investment rate and remained constant at about 20 percent of GNP. As a result the current account remained approximately in balance. But in the early 1980s, the national saving rate fell, largely because of bigger government budget deficits. The resulting net saving deficit led to higher real interest rates, the appreciation of the dollar, and the associated current account deficits that emerged in the early 1980s. In the second half of the 1980s the budget deficit turned around somewhat, interest rates and the dollar fell, and the current account deficit began to narrow.

So it's primarily *macroeconomic developments* that explain the worsening of the U.S. trade balance in the early 1980s followed by its improvement later in the decade. To keep the trend of improvement going in the long run, we'll need further macroeconomic policy adjustments. Ideally, we'd accomplish this through either a fiscal contraction or an increase in private saving. Less ideally, we could accomplish it through a reduction in domestic investment. The current plans for reduced federal budget deficits are in the right direction.

In conclusion, I think the U.S. is in reasonably good competitive shape. U.S. exports have boomed and the trade deficit is lower than it was in the mid-1980s. More important, measures of labor costs and productivity, particularly in manufacturing, indicate resurgent U.S. price competitiveness. U.S. productivity growth in the 1980s has been comparable with and, in some cases better than, other industrial countries abroad. The continued existence of U.S. trade deficits reflects an imbalance of national saving below investment, not any fundamental decline in U.S. international competitiveness.

Of course, when you talk about competition, you're always talking about winners and losers. And there's no question that some industries are going to continue to face difficult times from foreign competitors. But the real winners will be consumers for whom foreign competition means better quality U.S. products. The experience of the U.S. automobile industry is a case in point. Moreover, in a dynamic competitive world economy, with new products, technologies, and production processes continually becoming available, there will always be some firms on the decline as others are on the rise. The appropriate policy response to an industry that's losing ground to foreign competition is not to erect barriers to imports, but rather to facilitate the redirection of workers who lose jobs to more productive employment opportunities elsewhere. If the protectionist route is followed, newer, more efficient industries will have less scope to expand, and overall output and economic welfare will suffer.

And this brings me back to the main question of this conference: U.S. prosperity in a competitive world. The real issue of our long-term prosperity, of maintaining and improving American living standards, doesn't depend on how stiff the competition is abroad. It depends primarily on our *own* productivity growth and our ability to maintain a stable economic environment. The Federal Reserve has a role in this, of course. And that is to conduct a low-inflation monetary policy. But that's not enough. This country also must grapple with the hard issues of devising the means to boost productivity—

☐ with policies that foster greater private capital formation,

☐ with policies that increase investment in infrastructure,

☐ with policies that expand research and development expenditures,

☐ with policies that improve the quality of education,

☐ and with policies that stimulate entrepreneurial activity.

To sum this all up: Our prosperity doesn't depend on distorting markets with industrial policies and protectionist barriers; instead it depends on improving our productivity and letting markets work to bring out the best in our natural and human resources.

Thank you.

QUESTIONS FOR ANALYSIS

1. Professor Krugman seems to fear that a trade war may break out between the United States and Japan. Why?

2. If a trade war were to break out, would it matter? Why or why not?

3. If the United States has a comparative advantage in the production of pharmaceuticals and if Japan has a comparative advantage in the production of autos, what are the advantages in the U.S.'s specialization in pharmaceuticals and Japan's specialization in autos?

4. If the United States has a comparative advantage in the production of pharmaceuticals, can we be sure that the United States will be an exporter of pharmaceuticals? Why or why not?

5. Mr. Lutz states that: "Last year . . . the European Community told Japanese automakers that they can have no more than *16 percent* of the European auto market through the end of this century." What groups gain from this policy, and why? What groups lose from this policy, and why?

6. Mr. Lutz goes on to say that "the Europeans have basically said that their key, strategic industries, including autos, and the jobs that they represent are *important* to them . . . [B]y and large, they have, in my opinion, found a much better trade-off than we have between the so-called 'rights of the consumer' and *also*-very-legitimate rights of those very same citizens to be gainfully employed." Why does Mr. Lutz believe such a tradeoff exists? Do you agree? Why or why not?

7. According to Mr. Lutz, "earlier this year General Motors, Ford, and Chrysler had contemplated filing a dumping charge against Japanese automakers . . . (And we're talking about cars being dumped for as much as $5,000 below their prices in Japan. So, this was no inconsequential matter.)" What is wrong with Japanese automakers selling their cars in the United States for $5,000 less than in Japan?

8. Mr. Parry does "*not* think that the trade deficit is due to lower wages, superior technology, and 'unfair' trade practices abroad. On the contrary, [he thinks] we can find the sources of the trade deficit in certain macroeconomic fundamentals—namely, our own government budget deficit and our investment and saving patterns." What has the government budget deficit got to do with our trade deficit? Is it true that our investment and saving patterns are related to our trade deficit? If so, explain in detail what the relationships are.

9. According to Mr. Parry, "I don't think the trade deficit is necessarily the best way to judge our competitiveness. There are more important factors to consider.

In particular, I would point to price competitiveness and productivity." Why are these factors important in this regard?

10. Mr. Parry concludes that: "Our prosperity doesn't depend on distorting markets with industrial policies and protectionist barriers; instead it depends on improving our productivity and letting markets work to bring out the best in our natural and human resources." Do you agree? Why or why not?

11. Mr. Parry points out that productivity in manufacturing grew more rapidly during 1985–92 in the United States than in Japan, Germany, or France. Does this mean that productivity in the entire economy grew faster in the United States than in these other countries? What are the problems in measuring productivity in industries producing services? Will the rate of productivity growth be increased by policies that (a) increase private capital formation, (b) expand research and development expenditures, (c) improve the quality of education?

12. What can the federal government do to (a) increase private capital formation, (b) expand research and development, (c) improve the quality of education?